GLENN FORD

RFD

Beverly Hills

GLENN FORD
RFD
Beverly Hills

GLENN FORD *and*
Margaret Redfield

HEWITT HOUSE *Old Tappan, New Jersey*

To all my homegrown friends

Contents

1   I Say It's Spinach   11

2   One for the Cutworm   15

3   You Have to Tell Them Good Morning   19

4   What About Your Image?   25

5   But Is It Deductible?   29

6   Meanwhile Back at the Ranch   33

7   Murder Most Fowl   38

8   Ill-Met by Moonlight   42

9   More Truth Than Poultry   46

10   Life With the Lesser Peach Tree Borer   49

11   A Various Language   52

12   I Really Dig It   56

13   That's Why They Call It Truck Farming   60

14   The Enemy Without   63

15   The Root of the Matter   69

16	Loam on the Range	73
17	Infinite Riches in a Little Room	79
18	Sauce for the Goose	83
19	A Mind Like a Suitcase	86
20	Cabbages Is Beautiful	92
21	Who's Minding the Store?	95
22	Fly Swatter, Anyone?	98
23	Making the Earth Say Beans	103
24	Snacktime in the Garden	107
25	One Touch of Nature	112
26	It Helps to Have a Sense of Humus	115
27	And Cast of Thousands	120
28	Bare Roof Oranges	126
29	Delicious! What Is It?	133
30	Thyme on My Hands	138
31	The Dangers of a Happy Childhood	146
32	What's Bugging You?	152
33	Good Guys vs. the Bad Guys	159
34	Worms, and the Rich, Full Life	162
35	Tell Me All About It	167
36	The Lowly Mushrump	174
37	Time Is a Gentleman	181

GLENN FORD

RFD
Beverly Hills

1   I Say It's Spinach

Back in the days when *The New Yorker* magazine was under the able and acidulous guidance of Harold Ross, a cartoon by Carl Rose with caption by E. B. White appeared, which I daresay was posted in more kitchens and stuck onto more desk blotters than any other cartoon in history.

It shows a small child staring morosely at a dab of something on the plate, as the mother says, "It's broccoli, dear," to which the kid replies, "I say it's spinach—and I say the hell with it!"

Any parent who has gone through the I-can't-eat-that-it-makes-me-sick stage with a child who sits wanly or tearfully at the table, turning his head away from anything resembling a vegetable, has an instant rapport with that cartoon.

It might have been inspired by my son Peter.

I had fairly stable ideas about his diet and tried with about average success to make allowances for the normal antipathies children develop toward foods that are supposedly "good for you." But generally speaking, I felt that a child should eat what was put before him, and avoid making unattractive noises over the things he didn't care for; in short, to "behave mannerly at table, at least as far as he is able," to quote one of Robert Louis Stevenson's less inspired verses.

But it became more and more difficult to cope with the sight of a small boy apparently preferring death by starvation unless he was assured a 100 percent vegetable-free diet.

I wavered from one theory to another, as advanced by friends, family, and child specialists: one, he was being stubborn and capricious; two, he was enjoying the attention; three, he was a victim of some obscure neurosis or vegetable trauma; and four, what he needed was a father's hand—right across the seat of his pants.

In addition to the vegetable antipathy, he carried in his mind an agony list of meats, which took in virtually everything but hamburgers. I overcame this, more or less, by the psychologically unethical, but effective method of saying of practically anything protein except eggs, "It's buffalo meat, and Daddy shot it."

Oddly enough, the fact that the product before him had been rendered defunct by Daddy was a guarantee of its acceptability. In this way I was able to get veal, pork chops, lamb, and even liver and kidneys, into his prejudiced digestive processes.

One of the advantages of being a motion picture actor, and particularly one who makes a lot of Westerns, is that you may quite legitimately claim to have encountered a plethora of buffalo meat on the hoof.

Peter should probably have been born in the days when

man shot his dinner, caught his breakfast in the brook, and gouged his living out of the unwilling earth. Like Miniver Cheevy, "Born too late . . . he missed the medieval grace of iron clothing."

Fish, served pallid and boneless on a parsley rimmed platter, revolted him, until it became "salmon that Daddy caught." Here Fantasy rubbed elbows with Truth, because it has been my custom over the years to go each summer to British Columbia to fish for salmon on the Campbell River, and a large quantity of the catch is smoked and frozen for winter use.

But vegetables were an insuperable obstacle. We tried dressing them up, and down; we chopped, creamed, boiled, baked and french fried. We carved faces on carrots and turnips, and featured animal crackers in the vegetable soup —with no success. I tried to be understanding, but it was hard, because I can honestly say I have never met a food I didn't like.

One day I said, more in desperation than in hope, "Let's you and I plant a garden, Pete."

He said, "Okay, sure!"

The next day I brought home packets of assorted vegetables, radishes, lettuce, parsley, beans and corn.

Because radishes are the fastest germinating seeds, we put them in first. They were doing push-ups before they had had time to get comfortable in the bed.

I didn't realize it then, but the morning I shouted, "Hey, Peter! We've got radishes!" was the turning point. "Look there," I said, when he came running out, "Isn't that a great feeling? Our own radishes!"

"Gee!" he said, "I guess I didn't really believe they'd come

13

up." He pulled up one of the seedlings, and I didn't demur. I wanted him so radish-oriented that he would know them from infancy, right on into that magic moment when he could pull a full grown root from the brown earth, brush it off on his sweater sleeve, and hear the pleasant crack! as his teeth bit into it.

To Peter, the root vegetables were the most exciting, because they were nature's grab bag—reach down, pull, and see what the prize is. So we planted more radishes, carrots, turnips and potatoes.

Next we tried lettuce, parsley and beans.

Meanwhile, we ate radishes with everything but ice cream. I began to hope for a crop failure, but I need not have been concerned. Nature's balance wheels were turning . . . turning . . . the flea beetles were on the way.

2   One for the Cutworm

Meanwhile, Peter and I were seized with a desire to walk through our own personal corn field.

The only part of the yard allowing the amount of space we needed was in partial shade for much of the day. That was mistake number one. Mistake number two was our complete naiveté in the matter of nature's marauders. We were due to learn the homely truth of the old Indian rhyme

> One for the cutworm,
> One for the crow,
> One for the blackbird,
> And three to grow.

The kernels sprouted promptly, the sharp green blades knifing through the mostly adobe soil (mistake number three), some with the shell of the parent kernel impaled on the tip—a pretty sight.

On the third day after the first sprouts appeared, when we came out to inspect the corn rows, we found fully half of the green tips gone, neatly severed at ground level. Later we discovered that blackbirds were strafing the rows, tweaking off the succulent green tips, and nipping down far enough to get at the sprouting kernels. It was even-Steven between blackbirds and cutworms. One enemy worked above ground, the other below.

After that, until the shoots were stronger, we protected them with inverted flower pots, leaving them in place until the middle of the morning. These acted as little hot houses, the small drainage holes admitting just enough air so that the plants didn't sweat. We learned to spot the cutworms, cozily curled against the base of the shoots, resting after their hard night's work.

As the shoots grew into stalks, and the leaves elongated, Peter became as avid a corn watcher as he had been a radish inspector. It was just as well, since the radish leaves were beginning to be riddled with tiny holes, and the new crop, far from resembling the crisp, pungent well-rounded produce pictured on the seed packets, were as skinny and elongated as a Vogue fashion model.

But the corn seemed on its way to fulfilling all expectations. The time of restless waiting for the ears to form, the pressing, peeping and pinching to see if kernels were really there under the husks and the silk, was as exciting to me as to my son.

In a career which had precluded, or so I thought, any hobby as demanding as gardening, I had forgotten the morning joy of a before-breakfast tour to see what green wonder had manifested overnight.

The bean sprouts, still struggling out of their brown jackets, the parsley beginning to feather out, the ferny promise of carrots, all these were stirring a long forgotten interest.

Our enthusiasm was warmed rather than dampened by the twice-weekly pessimism of our gardener—something of a misnomer, since he was primarily a mower of grass, trimmer of hedges and occasional setter-out of plants which produced little but leaves and brief splashes of color.

To this day it drives me up the wall to waste planting space on things for show only, when there are so many plants that yield both beauty and provender.

Why plant birches, when peach trees give both shade and beauty, blossoms for the house, and fruit for the table? Why set out hedges of Eugenia or privet, when you can use guavas?

The gardener had watched our activities with an occasional pitying smile. One day, a little irked, I asked what he thought of our corn patch.

"Won't grow," he said, without stopping in his labors of "raking" the lawn with a hard spray.

"I know it's a little shady," I conceded, "but look at those ears."

"Wait'll you taste 'em!" shrilled Peter.

"Too shady," said the pessimist. He went on glumly watering the lawn, which was receding steadily due to the hard spray and our encroaching garden. He added a final pronouncement over his shoulder. "No kernels," he said.

We harvested a few weeks later. We had fourteen ears, with a yield of, roughly speaking, thirty-seven kernels to the ear.

A lot of soil has gone under the cultivator since then, but

corn remains my only consistent crop failure. (You'd think that having been associated with so much of it in my work, I would have developed some sort of a knack for it!)

I've planted it in rows and in hills; I've arranged it in "blocks" of three rows side by side, which experts say assists the pollination process. I have planted it early, in midseason, and late. The only thing I haven't tried yet is the old Indian system of "planting" fish in the hills for fertilizer. Thinking that the adobe soil in that first garden effort might be the problem, I took the gardener's grudging advice, and emptied fireplace ashes in it. ("Good for dooby," he had said briefly.) As time went on, my personal experience confirmed my opinion that the only thing that is good for dooby is to dig down twelve inches or so, throw out the dirt, and fill in with top soil.

One more thing I neglected to try. I didn't talk to the corn. Certainly with all those ears, it might have some affect.

Don't leave now! It is a scientifically established fact that not only are plants subject to emotions such as fear, apprehension and affection, but they are sensitive to the unspoken thoughts of the humans who work with them. And this sensitivity can bridge distances up to fifteen miles!

3 You Have to Tell Them Good Morning

I am only one of many people who believe that plants are sensitive to sounds. This theory is rather more recent than the one establishing the fact that music has a beneficial affect on the egg productivity of chickens. (No one as yet has come up with an album called *Music to Lay By*, but it may happen any minute.)

I am very careful—or I have been up until now—about expressing my theories on horticultural ESP. Still, I have done enough experimenting to know that, while music has charms to soothe the feathered breast, plants are even more responsive to the spoken word—and even to unspoken thoughts.

I have talked mine out of a drooping lethargy, and seen them literally turn over a new leaf at the very brink of the compost pile.

Personally, I see nothing absurd about it. Most of us in our city living have days when we seem to be almost physically assaulted by noise. And all of us know the therapeutic value of a retreat to the quiet of mountains or country.

I don't find it at all strange that plants, being living, breathing organisms, are sensitive to their environment.

This is not to suggest that I spend my off-hours out in the back yard crooning to the kohlrabi, but it is to say that you will see some remarkable results if you will make the effort to establish this sort of verbal rapport with your garden.

As I said, I kept pretty quiet about the whole thing until I came across a report by a well-established scientist, Cleve Backster who, through experiments with polygraphs (line readings), definitely established that plants respond to words of encouragement and also to situations of danger, rough handling and threats.

Backster's findings were first reported in *National Wildlife*, which may sound like an anthology of the best of *Playboy*, but is actually the name of an excellent magazine on outdoor living.

So try it on your cauliflower, one of these days. Like Shakespeare's soothsayer, you may discover that "in nature's infinite book of secrecy, a little I can read."

Certainly we need not be soothsayers in order to "read" the effects of our own attitudes and emotions on garden and house plants.

The late Allen Boone claimed that he could communicate mentally and verbally with Strongheart, the movie dog who was in his charge, and with the lower animals and insects as well. This is to report that I have had absolutely no success with cutworms, ants, mosquitoes and other pests. Either I am not getting through to them, or they prefer to ignore my signals.

As far as house plants are concerned, I have had great success with a sizable atrium. Roughly 24 by 18 feet, it is filled with a dozen varieties of trees and plants, ranging from philodendron to an eighteen-foot Kentia palm.

The planting area is on the ground floor, and the taller of the trees reach well above the ground floor level. Entrance to the house is on this second level, so that the tops of the trees are visible as you come into the hall.

It gives a junglelike effect, and first-time visitors have a tendency to hang over the wrought iron railing and peer down into the tropical greenery as if they expect someone in a pith helmet to pop out saying, "Dr. Livingstone, I presume?"

When I designed the atrium, or rather, expanded the original design, I violated, I am told, several rules for indoor planting—namely, the number and combination of plants, the distance from ground to skylight, circulation of air and the use of fluorescent lighting as an alternative to the chandelier suspended over the well.

Still, I have had good results, and I am frank to state that I think it is due to the fact that I talk to my plants.

They, in turn, demand certain courtesies. When they hear the click-splash of raindrops on the glass high above them, they like to have me turn on the indoor sprinkler to make the experience more realistic. Don't ask me how I know this. I just know it. I have a subtle rapport with them, and I am convinced that many other avid gardeners have a similar sensitivity, although they may be reluctant to admit it.

Of course you can overdo this empathy thing, and find yourself getting involved with the emotional problems of your plants. Unfortunately the writers of gardening hints don't take into consideration the Cleve Backster polygraph findings.

Take the matter of the stocks. We had planted both high double and column varieties, for color and fragrance and also because stock was the only plant we found on the charts that carried the notation, under PROBLEMS: "None."

Think of it. A plant without problems—*anything* without problems in our complex society.

They were getting ready to bloom in their customary lavish, carefree manner when Peter remarked one morning that "the stocks are looking terrible."

"Which stocks?" I asked nervously. The market had been on the jumpy side lately.

"The pink ones," he said.

"Oh. Those. Maybe they need more sun than they're getting. I'll take a look."

"I'll go with you," my son said. I didn't think he was looking his lighthearted self.

The plants were lying around in an acute state of melancholia.

"I just did what it said," Peter commented as I poked and puzzled over the limp, bruised-looking stems.

"What did 'it' say?" I asked.

"It said to hammer the stems, and that would make them absorb the water and last longer."

"I'd like to take a look at the book where you read that," I commented.

After some rooting around in the toolhouse, he returned with a pamphlet on "Flowers for Indoor Beauty." It said just what he had reported:

Pound stock stems with a hammer. They will absorb water
more readily.

I looked down at the flower bed and wished I had never
heard of Cleve Backster and his polygraphs. I knew the air
must be blue with the kind of thoughts and flower talk not
generally associated with these gentle nymphs of nature.

"This book is talking about cut flowers, Pete. You pound
the stems before you put the flowers in a bowl or a vase—
after you've cut them." It *had* to mean that!

"Oh," he said. "*Cut* them!"

"That's right. This foo . . . this writer, doesn't make it
very clear. He skips from flower care in general, over to
flowers for the house."

"It's okay to pound them *after* you cut them, though?"

"That's right. It's supposed to draw the water up into the
stems, so the flowers last longer."

I kept thinking there must be a kinder way. Obviously
that writer didn't know a polygraph from a polygon. The
stocks probably would have a few well-frozen words to say
on the subject, when they got their strength back.

The theory of plant sensitivity has inevitably engendered
some good-natured guffaws. But at the price of vegetables, I
don't think we have anything to lose by being courteous to
the artichokes, and giving a word of praise to the apricot tree
for an especially generous crop.

In all seriousness, why should we not feel a sense of responsibility for all growing things, and a joyful acquiescence
to this green demand?

We know the value of encouragement and kindness in our

dealings with people. It seems perfectly reasonable to me that it should be just as effective with plants.

I believe, with Montaigne, that there is ". . . a certain respect, and a general duty of humanity that ties us, not only to beasts that have life and sense, but even to trees and plants."

So keep a civil tongue in your head, or you may find yourself stuck with a lot of uncooperative vegetables and parsimonious fruit trees.

You have to tell them *good morning* if you want them to do their best.

4   What About Your Image?

In between crop failures and struggles with cutworms and flea beetles, I was getting ready to start a new picture.

By this time I was really serious about gardening. I had come to the conclusion that the only way to do a thorough, professional job was to throw out the old dirt and start from scratch. I was going to grow the finest produce in Southern California, but it was going to take a lot of work—and time.

In my business, making a decision is not a personal matter. It takes in a number of other people, and involves a lot of economics, mostly theirs.

I mentioned my new-found hobby over lunch at the commissary, with the studio publicist. Press representatives or publicists spend a lot of time sitting in their offices rubbing ideas together until they strike a spark. They are deadly serious about their work, which is people like me, because the image they build is either going to be a towering thing of beauty, in which event they can bask in its shade, or a plaster monstrosity that can fall and flatten you both.

The salad was 98 percent shredded lettuce, with a half-green tomato and a few status-symbol shrimp. It was the tomato that reminded me. "I'm going to raise tomatoes that wouldn't recognize this one as a sixty-seventh cousin twice removed," I observed.

"Raise tomatoes?" he said nervously.

"All kinds of vegetables. Kale and squash and lettuce and radishes . . . did you know that radishes are the fastest germinating of all vegetables?"

"Sh-h-h," he said, looking around apprehensively.

"What's the matter with raising vegetables?" I demanded.

"Your image!" he said. "What about your image?"

"*What* about it?"

"What about it!" he echoed, "You're supposed to be a big action man, hard-riding, taciturn, fast with your fists. What's your public going to think? How's it going to look, for you to be fooling around with parsley and kumquats?"

"I don't know how it's going to look," I said. "I just know how it's going to feel—and taste."

It opened up, if you'll pardon the pun, a whole new can of beans. Sometimes you get to thinking about getting out of the Hollywood thing, quitting while you're ahead, and getting into more constructive and satisfying work.

The words, FORD THE KUMQUAT KING drifted by my inner eye, like cloud formations past the window of a plane. They twisted in the wind of fancy and came past again in a different shape: "Parsnip Prince predicts big year. Corners produce market. . . ."

"Everybody's diversifying," I reminded him. "Lots of motion picture stars have outside interests."

"Look," he said earnestly, "you're the tall-in-the-saddle guy, remember? It was bad enough when you sneaked off to that cooking school in Paris, and began giving interviews about soufflés."

"Omelets," I corrected him. "And it's not just a cooking school, it's the Cordon Bleu. Some of the most sophisticated people in the world have taken that course."

He flinched. "Sophisticated" is a word highly suspect in the field of Western movies.

"Well, of course if that's the kind of image you want to project . . ." he said glumly. He went into some distressing details about people in the industry who had had the wrong kind of label pinned on them.

There was old-time movie star Lew Cody, for instance. Somewhere along the line, and through no fault of his own, he got tagged "The Butterfly Man." Cody was a two-fisted guy, but that name nearly wrecked him. He finally got himself invited to one of the WAMPAS dinners, the monthly bash at which the gentlemen of the press foregathered in those days, and threw himself on their mercy.

Because they *were* gentlemen, they took pity on the guy, and let him off the hook.

I still couldn't get worked up about the image thing. I didn't see anything esthetic or un-Western about digging out boulders with a pickaxe, which was what I was doing in the back garden in my spare time. I asked him if it would make him any happier about the survival of my Western image if I guaranteed to use only genuine horse manure.

We parted with a slight sense of strain, but he hadn't given up. The phone was ringing as I walked into the house.

"Glenn! Listen! Great idea!" he rasped. "How about hanging a saddle and spurs on a hitching rail in front of the house? Then, if it gets out about you and the rutabagas, it's all part of the outdoor image. I'll plant a couple items. . . ."

"Forget it," I interrupted. "No hitching posts, no phony plants. I'll handle my kind of plants, and you handle yours, but nothing phony. I mean it."

There was a short silence. "Oh, well," he said hardily, "don't get sore if word gets around about Ford and his tomatoes, and people get the wrong idea about what *kind* of tomatoes. . . ."

"It's a calculated risk," I said.

5   But Is It Deductible?

The topsoil arrived and became a minimountain at the bottom of the yard. Peter and his friends played cowboys and Indians all over it, so that spreading it began to be less of a problem than keeping it all in one place.

The gardener looked sourly at it and developed a severe sacroiliac condition.

"As soon as I get time," I promised, "I'll begin digging out the old soil."

Meanwhile I was about to start a new film, *The Violent Men*.

I had gotten into the habit of carrying a paperback edition of a book on some aspect of gardening to read on the set during the waiting periods. The current one was a three-hundred-page tome dealing with soil types.

I was surprised to find that there were ten thousand types of soil in the United States. I was learning words like "tilth" which refers to tilled soil, and "crumb structure," and "platy."

The more I read, the worse my soil began to sound. The experts made a distinction between "natural soil" and soil that had been "mucked about," adding ominously that some "are structureless . . . single grain, . . . or massive. *Both of these extremes must be avoided.*"

I was now convinced I had soil that was afflicted with one or both of the extremes.

I was sitting in a quiet corner of the set waiting for a camera set-up, and brooding on the decadent situation in my yard when one of the bit players strolled over. "What's the book about?" he asked. "Oh . . . mostly dirt," I said, ". . . tilth, that sort of thing." I thought I might as well begin tossing off a few technical terms.

He leered. "Dirt, huh?"

"Yuh," I said, taciturnly.

He dug me in the side with a buckskin elbow. "I *knew* you was the real stuff," he said admiringly.

I got up. "Yuh, sure," I said. I strode off, trying to look two-fisted.

It was about a week later that I got a call from my business manager. "What are all these bills from the nursery?" he wanted to know. "A ton of topsoil, ten hundred-pound sacks of steer manure. . . ."

"I'll come in," I said.

An actor can write off some fairly surprising things, as long as the expense is necessary in his work. He can, for example, deduct the cost of riding lessons, if he must have that ability for specific films. He can write off shooting lessons, if a role demands expertise in the handling of guns. Swimming, fencing, dancing lessons, all are deductible if he is using those skills to earn his living.

Lessons in a skill he merely hopes to use are not. In short, specific training for a definite role is deductible, but self-improvement does not come under that heading, nor do hobbies.

I had a couple of days off before I went on location, so I went in the next day. He had a stack of bills in a bulky folder on his desk. I was a little surprised at how high the stack was.

I explained about Peter and vegetables, and the success of the raise-it-yourself project. "It's not deductible," he said.

I assured him that I was not merely indulging a whim. I was doing it primarily for Peter, of course, but I was discovering in the process that there was something in me that reached out to the bucolic.

"What's so far out about farming?"

"Don't call it farming," he said, wincing. "You'll get into a whole different area there, with government regulations and forms filled out in triplicate." He broke off and tapped the pile of bills with a nervous finger. "I didn't realize you were going into this thing on such a large scale. What about your work? You're liable to be making a picture halfway across the world in a few months, and what good's a vegetable garden going to do you then? Your career's the thing."

"I might pass up a few pictures," I said, "and enjoy my home and my family—and my garden."

"You don't want to go passing up a good picture just to stay home, bogged down in fertilizers and potting mixes," he said, looking morosely at bills featuring those materials. "After all, you're not getting any younger."

I gave him Groucho Marx's quip. "Do you know anybody who is?"

Agents and business managers are great on reminding you

of your mortality. Not only corporeal mortality, but career mortality. By the very nature of their work, they are given to gloomy predictions and solemn warnings. Over the years, most of them have compiled some graphic instances of what happens to stars who live it up instead of putting it up, or who turn their backs on opportunities, just to get away from it all. It's a sort of verbal buckshot they keep on hand to shoot down their clients' flights of fancy.

I pointed out facetiously the similarity of terms in the fields of finance and agriculture. "Look how many slang terms for money derive from the vegetable family. Lettuce, long green, cabbage, kale, bean. . . ."

He didn't smile.

I reminded him that farming is one of the basics, a creative urge that goes back to Adam. I even pulled Emerson into the conversation, quoting the Sage of Concord to the effect that "all historic nobility rests on possession and use of land."

"I possess an acre and a half. Now I want to use it."

He listened with that weighted silence with which business managers have been assessing their clients' financial benders ever since there was a Hollywood. "Keep a record of any out of pocket expenses," he said when I was finished.

At the door, I turned. "Listen, have you *priced* vegetables lately? I paid twenty-eight cents for three skinny parsnips the other day. I can buy a whole package of seeds for twenty-five cents, and grow all I want!"

"It's not deductible," he said gloomily.

6 Meanwhile Back at the Ranch

I suppose I am as animal-oriented as the average man. I had a German shepherd dog a few years back, but he decimated the cat population over at James and Pamela Mason's place to the point where I had to either give him away, or lose their neighborly regard.

I haven't gotten another dog because my work takes me away a lot, and I think it is inhumane to leave pets for long periods, since, as the dog psychologists have pointed out, they have no way of knowing whether you're ever coming back.

How psychologists know this hasn't been explained to my satisfaction. However, we have poked into practically every other aspect of behaviorism, so I guess it is reasonable to believe that we can now figure out what a dog is thinking.

I confess I like to hunt. On the other hand, it disgusts me to see trophies mounted and displayed on the walls.

I don't kill anything I can't eat. I like deer hunting, and

make, if I may say so, a great venison, pork and kidney bean meat loaf.

When I first moved to Beverly Hills, it was dedicated to privacy, beauty and quiet. Always a close-knit community, it has since dropped a few stitches, but still retains a neighborhood feeling in a world which is more and more inclined to look askance at its neighbors.

We have what we consider the finest police force extant, and there is actually an anti-noise ordinance, "strictly enforced," according to the sign over Olympic Boulevard, where nobody would be likely to notice an extra bit of bedlam, anyway.

When I first moved there, there was a good deal of open country where the hills rose just behind our property. Foxes, racoons, coyotes, opossums and deer made their homes in the wooded slopes. Usually they kept to themselves, but occasionally a few malcontents wandered down, and those of us who lived in that area could, on moonlit nights, watch the deer nibbling on our expensive shrubbery.

When I came back from location, someone had given Peter two baby chicks. They were secondhand, actually, and like a lot of secondhand articles they showed a certain amount of wear and tear.

They had been an Easter gift to a buddy of Peter's, from some well-meaning but insensate relative. Peter took them in on a trade.

It was a good arrangement from a number of standpoints—especially that of the chickens. Peter had a certain amount of natural responsibility, which guaranteed the comfort and safety of anything entrusted to his care.

He had never been keen on eggs, and I felt that homelaid

eggs might prove to have the same appeal as the homegrown vegetables. All in all, I was glad to see his interest in the delapidated chickens. They were living in a birdcage that had once housed a pair of lovebirds.

"We'll build the right kind of house for them," I promised. I always liked to plan some sort of father-and-son project between pictures, to make up for the long stretches when shooting schedules left me little time with my family.

I can honestly say that if I were to find myself on the traditional deserted island, I could build a house that would stand up against the elements. When I first decided that I was going to be an actor, my father said, "That's fine, but first you're going to learn a trade, so you'll always have it to fall back on."

Thanks to him, I know something of carpentering, a good deal about electrical installation, and am a fair mechanic. Another thing he insisted on—before I could own a car, I had to know how to take an engine down and put it together again.

Peter and I set to work on the chicken pen with a roll of wire, some two by fours, and an enthusiasm that was about to get us into big trouble.

The pen was not what is called "functional" by commercial standards. Today's hens never set foot on the ground. They live in high-rise prisons with wire flooring through which their droppings fall, in the interests of sanitation, and the hell with the chicken's comfort. Even the eggs have gone modern. Instead of emerging onto a nest of clean straw, waiting for the farmer's hand to transfer them to basket or bucket, they are laid on the wire flooring, and roll down little ramps, into a receptacle below.

I don't look on hens as mere egg machines. I think they deserve some reward for what they do for a living, and I resolved that these should be able to take dust baths, cuddle down in clean straw when they felt an egg coming on, nibble on clover and kitchen scraps in addition to conventional chicken feed, and generally enjoy life.

When we finished, we had a pen roughly 20 by 40 feet, open at the top, with nest boxes along two sides (with an overhang to protect them) and graduated perches to accommodate the tenants at all stages of development.

We lacked one important item—straw for the nest boxes.

I discovered that straw is a commodity not to be found in Beverly Hills. After a number of calls to nurseries and hardware stores, I thought of a friend of mine in the San Fernando Valley who kept horses. He would have straw.

Before we left, we put the two chickens in their new quarters. They stood around looking surprised for a few minutes, then they discovered the joys of scratching in the dirt. "They look kind of lonesome," Peter commented.

Two hours later we were on our way home from the Valley, with the straw, and fifty white Leghorn hens and a rooster.

It had turned out that the next-door-neighbor of my horse-owning friend raised chickens.

"We won't have to spend a lot to feed them," said Peter, who was developing a practical side. "They can eat all those worms we'll find when we start digging out the old dirt."

"I don't want them eating the worms," I replied. "Worms are very valuable for the garden. They aerate the soil, and add nitrogen to it. Anyway, let's not worry about what we're going to feed the chickens. Let's worry about what we're going to tell the neighbors."

I was about to find out that a station wagon full of squawking chickens all trying to choke themselves to death by sticking their necks through the crates takes some pretty fancy explaining.

7 Murder Most Fowl

We began averaging a dozen eggs a day. While this seemed a small output considering the number of workers, still, roughly eighty-four eggs a week can begin to pile up.

The effect on Peter was what made it all worthwhile. His antipathy toward eggs vanished. He was up at daybreak, checking the output and rallying the girls to greater efforts. He ate eggs fried, boiled, Benedict, devilled, coddled and Foo Yung.

We began sending the overflow to friends and neighbors, which probably accounted for the latter's patient endurance of the rooster's sunrise song.

Then, overnight, tragedy struck. Peter came running in early one morning, pale and on the verge of tears.

"Something killed one of our chickens!" he burst out.

It certainly had—all over everything. And if there's one thing messier than a chicken that has met its end by assassin or assassins unknown and in one hell of a hurry, I can't think what it is.

It's awfully hard to get attached to a chicken. I think it's because you can't look them in both eyes. You can stand on one side and look in one eye, and then go around and look into the other, if you have the time, but you can't really communicate with a chicken as you can with a dog, even if you're so inclined.

Even so, we had a feeling of outrage. There was something that got to us—an indignation—to realize that a predator could violate this peaceful domestic set-up. What was it, we wondered, a neighborhood dog? An oversized cat? When I was a boy, we once had a dog that sucked eggs. I can still recall my father's disgust at the discovery. Next to a sheep-killing dog, an egg-sucker was the lowest form of canine life, although I was never sure just why this was considered a depraved appetite.

Maybe, I theorized, this was the work of a local egg-sucking dog, surprised at his work.

We had not put a roof on the pen, compromising by using an overhang on the side where the nests were. We liked having the top open so that we could come out in the mornings and lean on the railing to watch this feathered Utopia. It was about the closest my son's generation was likely to come to the days when you could lean over a hog pen and scratch the sow's back with a stick.

There was a peacefulness about that sort of thing, reminiscent of Whitman.

> I think I could turn and live with animals,
>   they're so placid and self-contain'd,
> I stand and look at them, long and long.

39

At today's pace we don't have time to stand and look at anything "long and long," and I'm not sure that farm animals are placid and self-contained anymore.

Even cows don't have the relaxed look they once had. Eyeing you over their shoulders as you whip past on the highway, they have a look of impermanence, as though they hear afar the sound of bulldozers getting ready to cement the pasture and turn the arable land into a housing development.

If some smart promoter would tape the nostalgic farm sounds—the gulp-gulp-gulp-wHoosH of a pump, the lowing of cows bound for the milking shed, the pensive clucking of hens in the barnyard, and the far-off bark of a rabbit-chasing dog, he might have a winner. It would be great for playing as you maneuver the five o'clock freeway traffic.

Peter and I couldn't figure out why we hadn't heard the noise of this fowl play. Certainly chickens are not the most self-contained members of the animal world. A bumblebee peacefully bumbling across the chicken yard can send them into hysterics. But we hadn't heard a thing. It had to be the work of some nondomestic animal, one versed in the sneak attack, silent and malevolently efficient. I thought at once of coyotes, whose sharp yapping we could hear sometimes when the wind was right.

We decided that we must extend the overhang, which gave the chickens shade, into a proper roof. But it would have to wait until the weekend. Meanwhile, we would keep alert.

The next night, at around eleven o'clock, I heard a muffled squawk from the vicinity of the hen house. Peter was asleep, but I shot out the back door, and raced across the yard just in time to see what at first sight looked like a large dog.

He scrambled up the wire fencing, and more or less poured himself down the other side and over the garden wall, carrying a limp chicken in his jaws.

He was the biggest grey fox I had ever seen.

That settled it. The next step was a stakeout in the best Dragnet tradition.

8   Ill-Met by Moonlight

I don't know whether or not you ever spent an evening in an elm tree. If you have, you must have had an interesting reason for doing it, because it's not a thing to be undertaken for the love of nature.

Elms don't give a damn about humans, anyway. They don't yield fruit and they cost a fortune in upkeep. If you don't keep their drooping limbs properly pruned, they snatch at you with sticky, serrated leaves as you walk by. In addition, they are subject to blights of a particularly unattractive nature, including cockscomb gall, sawfly, scurfy scale, phloem necrosis and Dutch elm disease.

If you ever climb one, you will discover that their bark is even worse than their blight. For taking the hide off of any part of you that you're fool enough to expose to it, the elm tree has no peer.

It was, however, the best vantage point in our yard, for airborne fox hunting. At nine o'clock on a moonlit night, I swung, scrabbled and cursed my way into its unwilling arms.

I intended to outfox the fox, and I had a twelve gauge shotgun to prove it. I'm not sure now whether my original intent was to let daylight through him or scare the daylights out of him, but as I look back on it, I suppose it was the latter.

My housekeeper took umbrage when she saw the shotgun. She stood on the terrace as I began my ascent, making remarks about grown men maiming little woods creatures, and other womanly comments.

Peter was on my side, and had to be restrained from following me up the tree, and was only momentarily placated by the privilege of handing the gun up to me.

The safety of the little woods creatures was not as important to him as the maintenance of his egg supply. As for my hunting skill, he had complete confidence in it, and was already making plans to cure the hide of the prey, and make fox stew out of the meat. I suppose he figured that a man who could bring down buffalo on the hoof with the stunning regularity I had achieved over the years would consider this night's work duck soup—or fox stew.

He was not a whining child, but he came close to it now. "Why can't I go too? I want to see Daddy shoot the fox!"

I did a little whining myself. "What's the matter he can't come along up here with me?" I foresaw a long, solitary night ahead, and the spritely presence of my son would alleviate the monotony.

We had been, after all, partners in grime throughout the whole grubby business of building the hen house, digging the postholes, making nest boxes and cleaning up after the tenants. I saw no reason for refusing to let him help protect the fruits of our labors.

"It's his bedtime," the housekeeper said promptly.

Personally, though I am a systematic person, and think regular hours are important in the life of a child, I believe there are exceptions. If a night is outstandingly beautiful, I don't believe the loss of an hour or two of sleep will stunt his growth. If baby chicks are due to hatch on a school morning, I don't feel that staying at home to observe this gentle miracle is going to have a lasting effect on his grades.

"Little we see in Nature that is ours," said Mr. Wordsworth. If his words were true in his time, their veracity is quadrupled in ours. But Peter went to bed, and I sat up in a tree by myself, because custom is a powerful force.

I sat and sat, endlessly—or so it seemed, after that part of me lost all feeling. I tried shifting about, to relieve the monotony and the impress of the elm bark. I shrugged my shoulders and flexed my fingers. I took deep breaths. Still I found myself nodding from time to time. I began saying over my lines from the script I had been studying. Anything, to keep awake.

After a period which I estimated to be some three hours later, I looked at my watch, and found that it was exactly forty-three minutes since I had made the ascent.

It was at that moment I heard, or sensed, as they say in mystery novels, that I was not alone.

The word "alone" is used here in its relative or broad sense. As a matter of fact, I was surrounded by neighbors, my family, and fifty-one white Leghorn chickens. What bothered me was that I was no longer alone in the tree.

Something had stealthily materialized out of the night, and was silently coming up the tree trunk. I was planning to leave just as silently, only faster, when I heard a hissing noise.

"Psst! I brought you something to eat!"

A small hand appeared through the branches just below me, thrusting a banana and peanut butter sandwich at me.

"She's asleep," Peter explained in reply to my unspoken question.

With that comfortable acceptance of a situation without needless comment, which is the essence of masculine companionship, we settled down to watch together.

At ten o'clock we climbed down. We were getting intolerably sleepy, and short of tying ourselves into the branches (a remedy Peter would have accepted with enthusiasm) there was no way of insuring ourselves against falling out of the tree.

"Tomorrow night, huh?" he whispered, as we parted in the hall outside his door.

9   More Truth Than Poultry

I prowled around the house a while. I was thoroughly awake now, whereas I had been almost staggering with sleep when I came in. I got a glass of beer and some cheese crackers and sat in the kitchen munching and leafing through the script.

Finally I took my gun and the flashlight and padded out to the tree again. It was cold now; the temperature on a July night in California can drop sharply in a matter of one or two hours. I had put on an old hunting cap, and a woolen robe over my pajamas. When I was once more ensconced in the tree, which had not been as simple as the first ascent, since I had to carry the gun along with me, I had what seemed a great idea. I would tape the flashlight to the barrel of the gun, and thus get a good look where I was aiming.

I was ready for action, and contrary to the way those things usually go, I got it. There was a sudden flapping and squawking from the direction of the chicken pen, and a grey streak passed over the fence and made for the ivy bank.

I raised the gun, sighted and pulled the trigger. There was a *blam* that nearly sent me backward out of the tree. The quarry kept on going, not even bothering to drop the chicken. I had missed him by a good ten feet.

Dogs began to bark. Doors slammed, somebody shouted, "What's going on out there?" and the neighborhood lit up like a driving range. I climbed down and stamped toward the chicken pen.

Police sirens began to whine through the usually quiet streets. It suddenly occurred to me that I might be responsible, and that standing out in the yard in a hunting cap and pajamas, holding a shotgun, was not the sort of thing my publicist friend had in mind when he talked about the right image.

"Gee, Daddy," said a voice, from the window, "what a *dirty* trick! You said you were going to bed!"

"Shut up!" I hissed. "And turn out the lights!"

For a long time afterward, that was known as The Night of the Mysterious Explosion. I think there was even a small notice in a throwaway paper, noting that "mystery detonation rocks Beverly Hills."

The next morning, two of Beverly Hills' best rang the bell.

"Mr. Ford," they said politely, "we understand you keep chickens."

"Well, sir," I conceded, "you might say that—I mean, we do have a few out back. Not many—fifty or so." It sounded a tremendous figure, suddenly.

My thoughts were dashing back and forth, trying to devise the retort rational, if the matter of discharging firearms in the city should be raised.

"You can't do that, you know, Mr. Ford," the second officer said. "You are in violation of a city ordinance which prohibits the keeping of livestock within the city limits."

"By George! You don't tell me!" I said. "Never crossed my mind!" (It hadn't, either.) I raised my hand, to forestall any idea that I might not be cooperative. "I'll get rid of them immediately. Did someone report it?"

"Why, no," the first man said. "The officers who were checking out reports of an explosion last night saw the pens while they were looking around the back end of your property."

"By golly!" I said weakly. "What do you know about that?" (Not much, I hoped.) "By the way, did you find out what the explosion was?"

"Nothing so far."

"Shook us up quite a bit," I mentioned solemnly.

Peter and I got rid of the chickens the same afternoon. We went out to the valley and sold them back to the man we had bought them from for half price.

I don't know what the fine is for discharging firearms in the city of Beverly Hills, but I figured it might have been about what the chickens were worth.

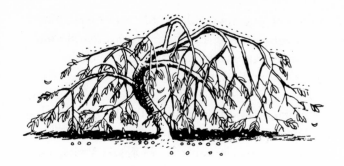

10 Life With the Lesser Peach Tree Borer

With the abandoning of the chicken project, I turned my attention back to the garden. I bought every book I could find on the subject of soil preparation, propagation and pests.

Today may be the age of the specialist, but in the world of seeds, weeds and floribunda, I figured I would fare better as a general practitioner.

How much better prepared I would be to cope, I reasoned, if I could learn to recognize the signs of the multitude of biting, sucking, web-weaving and egg-laying insects waiting in the wings for the show to begin.

In the process, I discovered that "the thousand natural shocks that flesh is heir to" just aren't in it with the varieties of afflictions that threaten the brightest and best of the earth mother's offspring.

As a dedicated gardener, it appeared that I was due to

deal with innumerable thrips, midges, mites and mealybugs, spittlebugs, pith borers, weevils and wireworms. Not to omit the diseases of wilt, damping-off, scab, mildew, canker and witches' broom.

And not all of them were to be found at ground level, or below. The really ingenious ones were up in the tree tops, or drilling away in the trunks, like the Lesser Peach Tree Borer. (The name implies that there must be a Greater Peach Tree Borer lurking about, but if there is, I'd just as soon not know about it.)

I sometimes wonder about those romantic gardens of yesteryear, glorious with color and fragrance. "Come into the garden, Maud, for the black bat, night, has flown. . . ." "A Garden is a lovesome thing, God wot!"

Nobody seemed to have found it necessary to warn the ladies, lovely in gossamer gowns and floating scarves, to "watch your skirts on the nasturtiums, Maud, they're full of black aphids." Or, "It's not the best time for a stroll under the pine trees—they're jumping with bagworms this year."

Of course, those were simpler times, and I think the plants and animals were less complicated organisms, too.

Some friends of mine recently bought an old house with an equally old and enchanting garden. In it was an aged grapefruit tree, loaded with fruit and dead wood, and growing in ground that had evidently not known the touch of hoe or hose for some time.

They went to work, pruning, feeding, and deep watering, all the while envisioning next year's yield, when the well-trimmed branches would be laden with golden fruit. Instead, the leaves began yellowing and falling off, and hundreds of pea-sized young fruit littered the area beneath the tree.

Horrified, they called the nursery from which they had bought the expensive plant foods and garden implements. Their distress was so moving, or they were such good customers, that the nurseryman offered to stop by on his way home that evening.

When he got there, they ushered him out to the garden, agitatedly repeating all that they had told him on the phone.

He heard them out, studied the wretched tree silently, then gave his professional verdict.

"What you got here," he said soberly, "you got a tree that's in shock."

They looked at him, smiling politely and waiting to hear the rest of the joke. But he was as serious as a squash vine full of pickleworms. Generally speaking, nurserymen are not given to looking on the light side. Life to them is a constant round of smog burn, petal blight and root rot. What's to laugh at?

"In shock?" my friends echoed, "This tree is in shock?" They were beginning to feel that way themselves.

The nurseryman circled the patient, prodding, chipping off bits of bark with his fingernail, rolling the fallen fruit between thumb and forefinger.

"Sure, trees can go into shock. This one hasn't had any attention for a long time; the roots were dried out, the soil was debilitated. Suddenly it gets a lot of nourishment, deep watering, some drastic pruning . . . don't be too upset," he added kindly. "Next year you'll begin to see the good results of the care you're giving it."

He was right. The tree is so loaded with fruit now, that the old, brittle branches are cracking under the weight.

11 A Various Language

William Cullen Bryant knew what he was talking about when he wrote:

> To him who in the love of Nature holds
> Communion with her visible forms,
>   she speaks
> A various language.

Propagation, according to the seed and soil experts, is the science of increasing plants from seeds and cuttings. It seems to me reasonable to assume that Impropagation is when you do it wrong.

At any rate, in my study of gation, both propa and impropa, I learned a whole new language.

"Dodder," for instance, doesn't mean merely the comfortable term it once did to me and Webster, i.e., "to shake, totter or potter." Dodder is also "a parasite that grows on stems and other parts of plants." (For informal occasions, it goes by the nicknames of Devil's Hair or Hell-bind.) "Lodging" is a condition of stem weakness which causes the plants to fall over in a strong wind; or being caught with your plants down. "Chrysanthemum Stunt," which sounds like a juggler with a potted plant act, is really a virus disease of that supposedly hardy perennial; "skeleton" is the physical structure of garden soil, and "frass" is a sawdust-like residue indicating the presence of borers.

I was learning also that today's gardener is up against some of the most ingenious, dedicated insects that ever got a foothold in the fungus.

In addition to outnumbering us, they are likely also to outsmart us. Out at the University of California at Los Angeles Stephen Bernstein, an assistant professor of psychiatry, has been making a study of ant brains. He has discovered that the ant's intellectual capacity corresponds roughly with the size of the brain, so that the bigger the ant, the smarter he is. A distressing thought.

Texas leaf-cutting ants even grow their own fungus for mushrooms of a sort, by chewing up leaves of crops.

For pure horror, forget the science fiction books, and the late, late rerun of *The Snake That Swallowed Wichita*. Just read up on some of the garden pests as described by the experts.

That charming little fellow, the inchworm, celebrated in song and story (undeservedly, it now appears), turns out to be the Spring Cankerworm, a caterpillar of which one report says solemnly, "in years of peak abundance, you can actually hear them eating, and are sure to collect them on your clothing while walking along the street." (A disheartening picture.)

I have not, I admit, heard caterpillars eating, and I devoutly hope this privilege is never going to be vouchsafed me. Neither have I, in my strolls through Beverly Hills, collected any on my clothes. Personally, I think the Chamber of Commerce should look into this thing, and see that it doesn't ever become a possibility.

The Eastern Tent Caterpillar sounds almost equally as alarming, and some authorities warn us sternly "not to attempt burning nests in the tree with a flaming torch. This is most injurious to the tree, and all too often brings out the fire department." (I certainly wouldn't want to get involved there.)

I was relieved to find that the "eastern" appellation meant he is indigenous to the area east of the Rockies, although the authority adds ominously, "at present."

As for the periodical cicada—which I at first took to be a grasshopper addicted to chewing up old magazines—the day it arrives (fortunately only every seventeen years) "the air is hideous with its continuous high-pitched whine, and oak trees look as if they had been suddenly struck by blight, being covered with twigs and small branches hanging down brown and dead." What a mess!

Night after night, I holed up in the study after dinner, trying to catch up on some of the reading that I felt would make me a more efficient gardener, and making copious notes. Gradually I began to wonder if it was worthwhile to plant anything.

I was reading some particularly heady stuff one evening, with graphic illustrations, greatly magnified. Feeling more and more pessimistic, I pressed on to the Buffalo treehopper, which sounded like a dance number from an old Busby Berkeley musical of the thirties. Under the picture was the comment, "It does somewhat resemble a buffalo in side view." It did, too.

I passed rapidly through the descriptions of the red-headed pine sawfly, onion maggot and carrot rust fly, the two-spotted mite and the codling moth, which in its worm form was reported to leave "dark masses of frass." I decided these things were better left unknown.

I closed the book and went out to the garden to stare moodily at the few fruits of my considerable labors. Listening uneasily for the whine of the periodical cicada, the gnawing of caterpillars and the drilling of the lesser peach tree borer, I heard only the sigh of the wind through the jasmine hedge, and the *flick* of a click beetle righting himself after losing his footing on the gravel.

I went back into the study, gathered up the books, and threw them into the trash basket.

"The hell with it!" I said. "I am going to enjoy this garden, regardless."

And I have, and am, and expect to keep right on doing it.

12   I Really Dig It

Dirt is the hardest thing in the world to get rid of. You can't sell it, you can't give it away, and it's illegal to throw it away.

I'd seen occasional signs in front of suburban homes reading FREE DIRT, and never could quite figure them out. Now I know. Some poor devil was in the mess I found myself in after I got the stuff dug up.

Once I had completed my Education of a Self-Made Gardener by throwing away the text books, I realized I had at last precipitated myself into the situation I had been subconsciously avoiding. I was finally going to have to get in there with a shovel and a pickaxe and start moving the earth.

I got up at 5:30 one brisk spring morning, and went outside determined to really put my back into it. When I straightened up an hour later, I thought that was exactly what I had done. I had staked out an area roughly twelve by eighteen feet, and was digging down to a depth of two feet. (I discovered later that you don't replace two feet of dirt with two feet of dirt. The first season's rain makes for a depletion of almost a foot, as the new earth settles—but that was a later problem.)

It would have been simple enough to get a man in there with a tractor, but I wanted this to be a home garden in every sense of the word. Just the same, I wished I had delayed it until Peter got back from his weekend in the mountains. There's something immensely sustaining about the wholehearted approval of an eight-year-old. Also, I was at the point where every bit helped, and even three or four spadefuls hoisted by my son would have made the job that much closer to the finish.

Even so, as the day wore on, I think I would have thrown up the spade and called the whole thing off, except for the fact that I had two loads, or fifty dollars worth of topsoil facing me, every time I wiped the sweat out of my eyes.

Just buying the soil had been a memorable experience. The nursery referred me to a man "who might be able to get it for you," which sounded like a line left over from prohibition days. When I called him, he didn't sound too enthusiastic about it. He was probably used to dealing with areas the size of Roxbury Park, and maybe this one wasn't worth his time. He wanted to know how many yards I wanted to order.

"Just one," I said modestly. "It's mine. . . ."

It turned out he didn't mean yard, as in backyard, but yard as in three feet. "How deep you gonna dig?" he asked.

I said, "Two feet?" The whole thing sounded so insignificant I almost made it six. "I want to plant an area about twelve by eighteen," I added, "Feet, that is." If I reduced it to yards, I was afraid he might get insulted at the low figure.

"What you want is eight yards," he estimated scornfully. "That's two loads. Twenty-fi' dollars. A load."

"Do you spread it?" I asked.

"Nah, I on'y dump it." What did I think he was? His voice implied. A day laborer? He was probably called a soil engineer. I don't know. You have to be careful what you call people today. The typewriter repairman's card reads CUSTOMER ENGINEER. Everybody's image conscious.

And now, here it was. Two loads, eight yards, fifty dollars worth, is a *lot* of dirt.

If necessity is the mother of invention, an aching back is the father. Along about three o'clock I got a great idea. I would dig down one foot, instead of two, then I would get some 2 by 12 foot boards and make a series of rectangular planting beds. The beds would sit one foot above the yard level, making it easier to work with, and the siding would conserve the soil.

The more I thought of the torrential rains we have in California—not just hard showers, but small cloudbursts as though someone up there was saying, let's get this over in a hurry— the more I realized that my good topsoil would be washed away.

These boxes, incidentally, are a good weekend project, as are the terrace boxes I use for sloping ground (to retain the soil). I use redwood because it won't warp, shrink or rot.

"What are you going to do with all that dirt?" the housekeeper wondered.

"I'll find somebody who needs some," I said, straightening up and leaning on my spade.

"If you don't want it, why would anyone else?" she asked reasonably.

When I knocked off for the day, between the mountain of topsoil, and the growing pile of old, or "sick" soil, as the nurseryman had labeled it, the yard was taking on the appearance of an archeological dig.

Something else that was increasing in size was the problem of what to do with all the dirt I was digging out.

I remembered that in *The Great Escape*, a group of prisoners tunneling out of the German prison camp were faced with the same problem. They solved it by stashing the day's accumulation of dirt inside their shirts. Then at exercise time, they walked around the prison yard dribbling it down their pants legs, a little at a time.

It made an interesting picture in my mind. I visualized myself strolling through the Beverly Hills parks, or sneaking down alleys, surreptitiously dribbling dirt out my trouser legs.

How long would it take to get rid of roughly four hundred and thirty-six square feet of soil? A man could get a reputation as an eccentric, that way!

13 That's Why They Call It Truck Farming

A wrangler friend of mine called me that evening with a question about the picture that was due to start shooting in another week.

A wrangler is the man who handles the horses, and what he doesn't know about them, nobody else needs to bother with. This particular wrangler, in addition to being a top man in his craft, is also a good friend of mine. It's just as well not to mention his name, considering the larcenous little job he was going to do for me with the studio truck.

"You got that pickup truck handy?" I asked, knowing he was going ahead with the advance company to the location site in a couple of days.

"Sure," he said.

"Can you get it over here tomorrow afternoon? I got a load of dirt to get rid of." I told him what I was doing, and the upshot of it was that he offered to come and help.

"Don't worry about the dirt," he said. "I'll take care of it."
What a friend!

He arrived complete with truck, spade and wheelbarrow. "Okay," he told me, "you keep digging, and I'll start loading."

I grunted my thanks, and started in again. When I looked around twenty minutes later, he had loaded the wrong dirt.

By the time we got that straightened out, and finished the digging, it was late afternoon.

"Where are we going?" my friend asked, as we slammed the tailgate and climbed into the truck.

"Where are we going!" I said. "You tell me. I thought you said you'd take care of everything."

"I said I'd take care of dumping it," he corrected. "It's up to you to say where."

I remembered a place out on Sepulveda, near the old golf driving range, long since high-rised out of existence. We roared out there and bumped onto the lot. Out came the shovels, down came the tailgate. Up came trouble.

"Hey! You!" somebody bellowed. A tough-looking character came striding across the field. "You can't dump stuff here, Mister!" he snarled, "This is private property."

"It's just dirt," I argued.

"Dirt we got!" he snorted. "Get your gear off my property!"

We got.

"Whyn't you tell the guy who you are?" asked my friend. "Nobody'd recognize you in those combat fatigues. He might of been glad to have a movie star dumping dirt on his property."

"And he might have liked to sue me for trespassing," I

countered. "I know a construction site they're excavating out Olympic. Let's try that."

Three hours, thirty-six miles and seven tries later, we rolled onto a vacant lot on Pico Boulevard and dumped the dirt. Nothing to it. It was eight o'clock, and pitch dark.

"I can't figure why you'd want to go to all this trouble," the wrangler commented reasonably, as we drove back to my house.

I explained. "The dirt was all played out—sick dirt—the plant nutrient content was practically nil, and the fertility level. . . ."

He shook his head. "Okay," he said. He drove along in silence for a while. "Boy!" he said at last. "And I thought dirt was dirt!"

He wouldn't come in. "I've been gone all afternoon and evening, as it is," he pointed out. "Besides, I'm not sure my wife will go for this story about sitting up with a load of sick dirt."

14   The Enemy Without

I was grubbing around in the dirt the next morning, when I had the feeling suddenly that someone was near me who was not filled with enthusiasm for my endeavors.

I knew who it was without looking around. It was George, my *then* gardener. I use the term to establish as firmly as possible, that it was not Fred, my *now* gardener. Fred is the best gardener I have had, and I hope he is going to continue to put up with my horticultural vagaries for many years.

But George not only had no faith in my abilities as a truck gardener, he was actively opposed to any efforts to increase the productivity of the ground, since that led inevitably to added labor on his part.

His hostility toward anything which blossomed or bore was so powerful that it preceded him through the gate like some infernal incense. At his footfall, tomatoes lobbed themselves over to the other side of the vine, and strawberries burrowed under the leaves like rabbits.

It wasn't that he gave any tangible indication of his antagonism. But there was a feeling in the air—I think it had something to do with the energy generated by his powerful thoughts about the work waiting to be done, especially where plants requiring staking, cultivating or feeding were concerned.

I picked up a book one day called *The Enemy in Your Garden* and was surprised to find that it was about insect pests, and not a biography of George.

Plants, like animals, know who their friends are. One look from George's leaden eye, and seedlings took down with damping-off disease, spinach plants broke out in mildew and tomatoes developed fatal cases of blossom-end rot.

Why, then, was he a gardener? Why not? No one seems to think it odd when people in other lines of work dislike what they do. In fact, people who really like their work are in the minority. "It's a living," the majority say, doggedly grumping through the week, dreaming of Saturday and Sunday.

A friend of mine who boards a bus at the start of the route every weekday, told me of the driver who climbed into the seat one morning, heaving a sigh as he pulled away from the curb. "Gotta hurry downtown," he grumbled, "so I can turn around and hurry back here."

As a matter of fact, people who go around singing on the job and proclaiming a love for their labors, are so unusual as to cause a certain amount of speculation among their colleagues. Let a teller take to whistling softly at his window, and the bank president is likely to turn pale and send for the auditors.

If a cook hums happily over the Beef Stroganoff, her employers start wondering uneasily if their next door neighbor has offered to double her present salary.

But people *expect* gardeners to be happy, singing about their work and chucking petunias under the chin at the drop of a hoe. Even the plants expect it, as Cleve Backster's polygraphs indicated.

George had a way of entering the yard with a slow, discouraged tread, as though each footstep said DOOM and GLOOM. It was expressive of the man's inner feelings.

He would stand for a long moment, looking slowly around the garden, then he would heave a great shuddering sigh, and get on with the mowing.

I blamed a good deal of my early gardening failures on sick soil, too much shade, and overwatering, but a lot of it was, I am positive, directly attributable to George. An attitude like his practically guaranteed crop failure. It got so I had to plunge out into the yard the minute he left, and talk the tomatoes out of a death wish.

On this particular morning I was cheerily turning my thoughts over with the sod, planning the vast agricultural project soon to cover the rich, loamy topsoil, when Peter joined me, eager to try out the new implement we had acquired. This was a dibble, a slim, pencillike tool with which to make holes or furrows for seeds. A pencil is just as good, and cheaper, but a dibble has the advantage of giving the whole enterprise a touch of professionalism.

"Look at our garden, George!" Peter called out. "We're planting beans. And then we're going to plant onions and squash and cucumbers and cabbage and carrots and parsley." He waved a hand in an expansive gesture. "We're gonna have millions and millions of vegetables and things!"

65

George grunted.

"Before we do that," I reminded Peter, "we have to get the rest of the place dug up." That meant ordering another load of topsoil, and going through the furtive business of disposing of the old dirt. With a new film in the offing, I wasn't too optimistic about getting the ground ready by green-up time.

Suddenly there came to me one of those lightning flashes of inspiration, so brilliant in concept and yet so obvious that I wondered that nobody had thought of it before. (They had, but I didn't know it at the time.)

I would put in a crop that would relieve me of the whole arduous job of digging out the old soil: alfalfa.

I had come across a brief reference to it in an alphabetical list in one of the garden books, and had been impressed by its glamorous past. Alfalfa has been around since 400 B.C. (I don't know where it was before that.) It first migrated from Asia to Europe, and in the sixteenth century some enterprising Spaniard took it over to South America. From there it went to San Francisco, evidently stopping for siestas along the way, since it took some two hundred years to make it from Chile to the Golden Gate, arriving in 1854.

My enthusiasm was generated by the fact that alfalfa roots extend more than fifty feet into the earth, where they reach stores of plant food other roots never get a crack at. Thus, when they have finished living on the fat of the land, or under it, they leave the soil full of rich organic matter, plus the benefits of water and air channels resulting from all that rooting around down there.

Unfortunately, that book was among those I had flung away so recklessly. I looked up alfalfa in the encyclopedia however, and was encouraged by its report that "the effect of alfalfa on irrigated land is to increase the value per acre of subsequent crops." The commentary ended there with a cryptic reference: "See Green Manuring."

Unfortunately we were missing the volume of GR-GU. I put in a call to the Farm and Home Advisory Bureau, which promised to send along the latest thoughts on alfalfa as set down by the University of California Agricultural Extension Service and the U.S. Department of Agriculture.

What I have always liked about the people at the Farm and Home Advisory Bureau is their matter-of-fact attitude. They don't take up your time wondering out loud how this G. Ford happens to have a working spread right in the middle of Beverly Hills. Their principal concern seems to be to get the required information into your hands as fast as possible—which in my case has always been the next morning. You get the feeling that Farm Advisors L. E. Francis and Lyle Pyeatt are behind you down to the last parsnip.

"Do you happen to know what green manuring is?" I asked George, who was diligently beheading pansies with the hard spray. "It's something to do with alfalfa."

He shook his head. "I dunno anything about alfalfa." (I got the impression he didn't want to know, either.)

"You know," I observed to Peter, "we just might put that whole end of the yard into alfalfa." I could see it undulating with the pleasant green of the "leguminous fodder plant" that was going to enrich our poverty-stricken soil.

George had evidently been doing some serious thinking about the matter, too.

"Mr. Ford," he said, "if you're figuring to go digging up this whole ay-rea, you gotta get somebody in here to do it

67

besides me. You know I got this terrible back. The shooting pains are something fierce lately, and I can't do no digging."

"It's all right, George," I assured him. "I think I'm onto something that will make it unnecessary for either one of us to do a lot of digging."

I went back to where Peter was dabbling with the dibble. "Hairy Peruvian," I muttered.

"What'd you call him?" Peter whispered.

"I didn't call him anything,"—though I could think of a few things. "I was just talking to myself, thinking out loud. Hairy Peruvian is the name of a variety of alfalfa I've read about, somewhere. It might be the kind for us."

Anything with a name like Hairy Peruvian had to have some gumption, and just might be the thing to put a little muscle into our sickly soil.

"What we have to find out," I told Peter, "is whether it's a variety that does well in this part of the country."

I tried to think back to the days of my youth on a farm in Canada. But my memory seemed singularly unencumbered by impressions from my agrarian past, possibly influenced by the fact that we had moved to Santa Monica, California, when I was five.

15　The Root of the Matter

The pamphlets arrived the next day. They were slim, mimeographed books with green covers—alfalfa green, probably—and covering every aspect of the business of alfalfa growing, from *Varieties Of*, to *Methods of Planting*, and *Pest and Disease Control Program For*.

I spread them about me on the patio table and ran my finger down the list of Nondormant-Southern Alfalfas until I found HAIRY PERUVIAN.

The variety, it seemed, was "characterized by hairiness on stems and leaves, and by rapid growth and quick recovery after cutting." That was what we needed—a strong, no-nonsense plant with hair on its chest, or the equivalent. I circled the paragraph with a red pencil, and then noted that "No certified seed of this variety is available." "Nor," I read further, "is any controlled genetic stock used for maintaining its identity." It sounded not only hard to come by, but a little mixed up, in addition. If there was one thing I didn't need, it was an uncontrolled variety hanging around the yard wondering who it was, like an unhappy teen-ager.

I dropped on down to the one called SONORA, which was reported as having "excellent resistance to the spotted alfalfa aphid" but didn't seem to have any fight left when it came to leaf diseases and the pea aphid.

CALIFORNIA COMMON 49, on the other hand was "tolerant to dwarf virus disease; less dormant than CALIVERDE but more dormant than MOAPA."

MOAPA sounded like the one for us. Not only was it described as resistant to the spotted alfalfa aphid, but it seemed to be able to cope with "several of the species of root-knot nematode." I marked it for my own, and went on to the booklet on *Method of Planting New Alfalfa*.

The seed bed should be firm enough to walk across and not sink below the soles of the shoes. Furthermore, where water leveling is used, the bed should be chiseled or spring-toothed four to six inches after it is water leveled. This is supposed to prevent compaction.

The whole thing seemed to be growing enormously complicated. All I wanted to do was to plant a fifty-foot area with alfalfa.

Sowing by airplane, while it sounded like a stimulating way to get the job done, wasn't too practical. Drilling, broadcasting or using a ringroller with a sowing attachment didn't sound like the answer, either.

It wasn't that there weren't plenty of alternative methods, it was just that they didn't quite seem to work in Beverly Hills. There was the matter of having the place "floated or land planed, so that harvesting equipment can be used ef-

70

ficiently." That sort of thing was going to play hob with the driveway.

It stressed the fact that the most successful plantings result from a well-prepared seed bed. That was where water-leveling, chiseling and spring-toothing were of such inestimable value. And the actual planting was even more colorful in its terminology.

In the Antelope Valley, I learned, it was usually done with a small disk-type drill, and drag chains on each disk blade, which seeded the field in a 4 by 4 inch checker-board pattern.

I began to regret having emphasized to Peter the importance of tenacity in any undertaking. I read doggedly on.

What I was doing was looking for a loophole.

While I was looking, I learned about SHEEPING OR GREEN CHOPPING, which I took to be involved with using sheep to cope with volunteer grain that was smothering the alfalfa seedlings. My sympathies were entirely on the side of the volunteer grain. I didn't mention any of this to Peter, who would have been happy to go into the sheep keeping business. I remembered with gratitude that the NO LIVESTOCK IN BEVERLY HILLS ordinance could always be invoked.

It took quite a while, but I finally found the loophole. It was smack dab in the middle of the last book in the pile.

Fall Planting is recommended and considered the most profitable time to plant new alfalfa.

"See, Peter?" I pointed out, "it's so important that they've even underlined it. Fall planting. This is Spring. We certainly can't let all this ground sit around doing nothing, waiting for the right time of year for alfalfa."

He saw at once the soundness of the decision. We would get on with the beans, squash, parsnips and carrots.

"Don't forget," the final paragraph in the *Method of Planting* booklet counselled, "tender loving care is important but too much of anything can cause adverse effects."

It certainly could. I had already felt the adverse effects of too much alfalfa, and I hadn't even planted any.

In some of the copious notes I had made during my nights of reading books on gardening, I had noted under MULCHES, that ashes from burned papers and garbage were full of phosphorous and potassium, and could be spread on garden or lawn, to good effect.

I thoughtfully laid the booklets in the grate in the den. I didn't like to waste them.

16 Loam on the Range

We got at it the next morning. We had decided on a combination of carrots and radishes in the first bed. (The original radish crop had long since been demolished by flea beetles, but we were wiser now, and richer in topsoil.)

The next bed would have tomatoes and cucumbers, and banana squash would have number three to itself, since it is a sprawler requiring plenty of space.

We had hardly gotten as far as making a dent with a dibble when I got a call from my agent. "I'll have to go down and sign some papers," I told Peter. "Why don't you go ahead and get the radish seeds in?"

I left him happily measuring the bed, in order to leave exactly half for the carrots. If there was one thing he was schooled in, it was precision. "Don't forget to leave enough room between rows," I reminded him as I backed out the driveway, "and don't plant them too deep. Three times the width of the seed is a good rule for that."

I came home two hours later, anticipating the inspection of the morning's planting. I could see Peter as I drove in, crouched over the radish bed, intent and diligent, a rewarding sight to a father.

"Did you get the crop in?" I called as I strode toward him. He turned his face up to me, and I was hard put to it to distinguish between him and a radish, as far as color was concerned. He was perspiring, red-faced and weary.

"I got seventeen planted," he said. He got stiffly to his feet. "Gee, I wish we could plant something that has *big* seeds—like beans or peaches or maybe watermelons. That would sure be a lot easier'n radishes." He started down the path, walking bowlegged. "My legs feel like they're full of cement," he complained. "I guess I shoulda stood up oftener."

I looked down at the planting bed. It was undisturbed except for a furrow perhaps ten inches long, tamped down to indicate the planting of . . . "*Seventeen radishes?* Peter! Come back here!" I called. "Did you say you planted just seventeen radishes? It took you two hours for that?"

I assumed that some of his friends had come by and talked him into going off on some more intriguing pursuit. Playing with his friends was fine, but not when he had taken on a job.

Another idea hit me. Great jumping gunnysacks! Could this mean a lessening of interest in the garden project? Were we about to return to the anti-vegetable syndrome, more dinner table scenes, and worries over nutrition?

I determined to be patient. "What I don't understand is how it could take all this time to plant just seventeen radish seeds? You sure you didn't go off somewhere with the guys, instead of finishing the job here first?"

74

"I didn't goof off, Dad, honest!" he insisted. "Chris came over for a while, but he helped me."

Chris was his best friend. An apartment house dweller, he was endlessly fascinated by our backyard farming activities. He was the one who, having heard from Peter of the value of dried blood as a soil nutrient, offered to stand where it would do the most good one morning when he cut his finger —thus becoming the only boy in Beverly Hills who was blood brother to a turnip.

"It's a *terrible* job to measure a radish seed!" Peter was complaining.

I must have looked stunned.

"You *said* they had to be planted three times the width of the seed," he reminded me. "So what we did was, Chris put three radish seeds side by side, and measured 'em. Then we planted 'em that deep."

"I meant approximately three times the width," I said weakly. "Just about. Not exactly."

"Well, anyway, it's a *terrible* job," he reiterated. "We didn't know it would take so long, or we wouldn't have done the surprise first."

"What surprise?"

He plodded wearily ahead of me toward the house. "It's not ready yet. Anyway, I'm awfully hungry."

We had a new housekeeper, Mrs. Kelly, who had started working for us just that week. She was a hearty, cheerful soul, with the build of a lady wrestler. I liked her looks, because she gave the impression of being able to cope with practically any emergency that was liable to occur on the domestic scene.

She trotted out some sandwiches for us, and we ate them sitting at the kitchen table, Peter being in no shape to go into the carpeted regions.

"What's the surprise you've got for me?" I asked again.

His face lit up. "Well, you know what you said about starting some seedlings in the house—in a box?"

"Mmph," I agreed through my sandwich.

"Well, Chris and I found this book out in the toolhouse. Remember when you bought all those books about how to grow things? We were trying to find something that tells how wide a radish seed is, and we saw this stuff about seeds indoors. We did just like the book said, and that's the surprise. It's almost ready," he added mysteriously.

Mrs. Kelly smiled approval over her ample shoulder. "That's the kind of a boy to have," she said.

She was doing something vigorous in a mixing bowl, and now she nodded toward the oven. "I think maybe a batch of my oatmeal cookies ought to taste pretty good about now." She started toward the stove.

Peter set his milk glass down with a crash. "Don't open the oven!" he bawled.

Mrs. Kelly leaped back. "Why not, for goodness' sakes!" she demanded, clutching her chest. (I could see she was having second thoughts about "the kind of a boy to have.") "What's wrong with the oven?"

"Nothing's wrong with it," Peter said patiently, "It's just, my dirt's cooking, and it hasta cook twenty minutes more."

Mrs. Kelly bent silently and peered through the glass oven door. Then she straightened and turned to look at me with a steely eye. It was the old guilt by association thing. "I don't know how a boy would get the idea of cooking dirt," she said coldly, "but I'm not going to work in any place where people don't know a stove from a hole in the ground."

Half an hour later, after I had done everything short of furnishing an affidavit guaranteeing dirt-and-boy-free kitchens, and after Peter had resentfully removed from the oven a large, flat aluminum pan full of soil ("It's got ten minutes more to cook, before it's done!") I went outside.

I found Peter moodily watering the row of seventeen radish seeds. I placed my hand on his shoulder. Sometimes it's better to say nothing, than to try to explain the vagaries of adults.

He sighed. "I shoulda done it the other way," he observed. "Then it would'a been out of the kitchen before she came."

"What's the other way?" I wondered. I was ready for anything.

"In the pressure cooker. It only takes fifteen minutes."

Just for the record, I went in and found the book. The page was marked with a radish seed envelope.

STERILIZING SOIL FOR INDOOR SOWING was the heading. It instructs you to fill a baking pan or roaster three or four inches deep, with fairly moist soil. Level off the dirt, and cover with aluminum foil. Then bake for forty minutes at 200 degrees.

For the impatient type, the pressure cooker method is recommended—fifteen minutes at fifteen pounds pressure.

That's what it said.

I was almost inclined to believe the writer of the book was being facetious—having a little innocent fun, a "dirty" trick on the gullible gardener, which would be explained in a later paragraph.

But it was on the level. As I have said before, writers on

gardening subjects are as a group an earnest, conscientious lot, not given to levity, and no wonder.

It is perfectly legitimate to sterilize soil in this manner, if you don't mind cooking dirt in your oven or pressure cooker.

Personally, I'm not keen on it.

17   Infinite Riches in a
Little Room

"What's your garden like?" people sometimes ask me, having heard that I'm a little haywire on horticulture.

It's reminiscent of the old vaudeville classic: "What's your wife like?"

"In comparison to what?"

At present writing, I have one hundred and fifty fruit trees, and every variety of berry and vegetable that will grow in Southern California, as well as some that won't.

I like to experiment. Not long ago I bought a basket of kiwi berries at the Farmers' Market. Since this product of New Zealand has never been grown here, I dried the seeds and planted them. I'm waiting to find out for myself.

My trees include orange, lemon, lime, grapefruit, apple, pear, peach, plum, apricot, fig, avocado, nectarine, tangerine, guava, persimmon and kumquat.

79

I have a pie-shaped lot that encompasses slightly more than an acre, which doesn't leave a lot of arable ground, since my fourteen room house and guest house sprawl over much of it. The land was once a part of the Louis B. Mayer estate. If there are such things as ghosts (which I firmly believe), there must be some lovely as well as ludicrous forms wisping about in the jasmine-scented air.

Perhaps the actor in me responds to the actor in the garden. It is, after all, nature's star performer. It plays multitudinous roles, and is constantly creating—good or bad, depending on the material it has to work with. But create it must. It is infinitely rewarding, asking only to give. This "givingness" is one reason I hate to see a vacant lot. I have bought lots and planted them with fruit trees, just to see the ground fulfilling itself.

Like the actor, the garden even has a profile to consider, since the layers of soil are collectively known by that name.

Much of my gardening has been by the trial and error method. In using all the arable space possible, I have learned to combine in the numerous planting beds, the fruits or vegetables that have similar tastes in watering and sunlight. Thus, cucumbers, tomatoes and boysenberries share one planting area—raspberries and strawberries another. Carrots are planted next to radishes, and against the back fence which divides my property from that of my good friend and neighbor, Rita Hayworth, Concord grapes grow side by side with Thompson seedless. (Rita and I have a reciprocal arrangement—she can pick my grapes, which hang over the fence, and I can enjoy her roses.)

I have surrounded my pool area with a high green wall of trees—at one end, myoporum, bamboo and jasmine. On

80

the east side, peaches and crabapples. I have never been able to bring myself to have the peaches cut back; in fact, pruning is a part of gardening I dislike to have done, and Fred, my gardener, is a happy man when I go away and he can catch up in that department.

I rarely buy seeds. I let a percentage of the squash, tomatoes and melons, for example, get almost overly ripe, then I open them and set them on trays in the sun, so that the seeds will dry. Incidentally, old window screens make excellent drying racks, not only for seeds, but for figs, which I like sun-dried.

Only about a quarter of my onion seeds are kept for planting. The rest I sprinkle in salads, dips or sandwich mixes.

I have found it better to start off with seeds, rather than plants. Transplanting, no matter how carefully done, is always a shock to the plant's root system.

I can't see planting lawns when there are ground covers much more beautiful and productive.

When the front of the yard was being landscaped, I had to go to France to make *Love Is a Ball*. When I came home, the area had been turned into lawn. I promptly had it taken up and replanted with strawberries.

My present crops include parsley, onions, eggplant, parsnips, kohlrabi, radishes, carrots, turnips, tomatoes, banana squash, watermelon, artichokes, summer squash, potatoes and lettuce.

If this garden can be said to have a theme, I suppose it is "Infinite riches in a little room." That line from Christopher Marlowe seems to say it well.

To me, the garden never loses its charm. I have come back to it from the horrors of Dachau and the fury of Viet Nam. I have returned to it from personal triumphs and bitter disappointments in people and projects. Its green welcome has never failed to lift my spirits and restore my peace.

There is no surer way, in my opinion, to work off rancor or to find quiet for decision-making, than to get out and dig and stake and cultivate.

Like a time-tested friend, a garden is as ready to rejoice with you as to comfort you. It is a respite and a refuge for those days when you are fighting the blues, or for the times when your heart hangs out a sign reading, TEMPORARILY OUT OF ARDOR.

18 Sauce for the Goose

In the years when I was growing up in Santa Monica, California, the Sunday drive was a family institution. At that time freeways had not been invented, and the little towns were separated by green miles of walnut and orange groves.

Now there are very few little towns, as such, most of the groves have gone, and sprawling smoke-belching industrial compounds hold the towns by grimy outstretched hands.

We used to drive along through the green and gold wonder of the groves, stopping at roadside stands for orange juice (ALL YOU CAN DRINK FOR A DIME), and vegetables, a penny a bunch.

In our neighborhood, nearly every house on the block had its fruit trees, and I was one of the nimblest fruit snatchers going. That line from the *Book of Common Prayer*, "Keep my hands from picking and stealing," was strongly applicable to me.

It's true that stolen fruit tastes best. To this day, I have never jumped anyone for swiping fruit from my trees. I figure it's one way of balancing the score for all those oranges and plums and peaches and avocadoes I used to pinch as I winged it down the alley.

My conscience was not overactive in those days, but when I reached the point in later years where the money was coming in at a reassuring rate, I began thinking of another area where I had committed some lighthearted larceny.

When I was sent to the grocery store, it was usually to a combination market and hardware emporium in our neighborhood. As I left with my legitimate parcels, I often made it a point to go out the back way, and palm a couple of potatoes from the bushel baskets by the door.

These were for roasting with a chosen few buddies in whichever backyard was least subject to parental inspection at the time.

Since then, I have eaten some memorable meals at some of the world's justly famous restaurants, but for sheer gustatory delight, nothing has ever eclipsed those potatoes roasted furtively and eaten on the run.

It can't be explained just by the "forbidden fruits" theory. The secret was in the method, which to me is still the ideal way to cook potatoes. We dug a shallow hole and made a wood fire hot enough to leave a good bed of ashes. Then we scooped a hole in the ashes, buried the potatoes, and covered them over with wet earth, over which we raked the hot ashes.

At any rate, when I achieved a state of advanced solvency as an actor, I often went out of my way to do my shopping at the store which had been the source of my potato roasts.

Later, when my fruit and vegetable crops made shopping

for those foods unnecessary, I began concentrating on hardware purchases there. I have, over the years, accumulated enough claw hammers, cold chisels, paint scrapers, rakes, hoes and saws, to open my own hardware store.

It has been a pleasant sop to my conscience to overbuy at the store where I lifted all those potatoes in my less scrupulous days.

As my career advanced, I have found it a great antidote for self-adulation, to stroll around in the old neighborhood, past the corner where I used to sell firecrackers, the drugstore where I washed windows, and the dry goods store where I swept out the stock room.

"Ya-a-a! Big shot!" they seem to say, derisively. It's a great way to keep your feet on the ground, and one of the advantages of spending your adult life in the same general area where you grew up.

19 A Mind Like a Suitcase

The best way to keep your memories green, instead of covered with blue mold, is to be selective about the things, both tangible and intangible, which you bring home from your travels.

The inveterate traveler has a mind like a suitcase. As he moves about, he is constantly cramming it with impressions, information and desires. Every once in a while, it's a good idea to stop and empty the suitcase, and decide just which of its contents are worth retaining.

Most of the things I accumulate while traveling can be fitted into one of three categories: ideas, kitchen utensils and rocks.

In the idea department, they generally can be applied to the house or the garden. When I first went to Finland, I became addicted to sauna baths. When I returned home, one of the first things I did was to add one on to my house. In Scandinavian countries the sauna takes precedence over everything else; when a house is being built, the sauna bath is the first room to be completed.

When I saw the orangery in the gardens of Versailles, I took home the idea of creating one of my own. In Japan, the terraced gardens at Kyoto gave me the idea of using the same system, in a small way, on a sloping section of my land. Using redwood boards, I devised planting pockets, or steps, and as a consequence, a whole area that once lay fallow now spills over with tomatoes, strawberries and artichokes.

One of the tangible things I brought back from Japan which doesn't fall into any of the three categories, was a bathtub, similar to the one in my suite in the hotel at Nara. Forty-two inches deep, it is like a miniature swimming pool. I installed it in the master bath (not without some qualms because of a Beverly Hills ordinance against bathtubs more than twenty-eight inches deep).

An international palate and a penchant for collecting cooking utensils can be terribly hard on your family or domestic staff. I have a marvelous couple who work for me, and who are endlessly patient with the things and ideas I bring back from my four or five trips per year. They are equally forbearing with the food phases I go through.

After I have been to Japan, I go on a shrimp kick; after Spain, I want omelets or paella, and France usually sends me home with a taste for escargot.

As for the utensils, I will use them for special dishes I like to prepare myself, but still must find the space to accommodate them.

Generally the utensils are things I can't buy in the United States: a wok, from Japan, for example. This is an iron bowl used to heat oil for tempura, and great for cooking scallops or for French frying summer squash or string beans, two favorites of mine.

From Morocco I brought back a Mongolian oven, which is a heavy metal cone, with small triangles of the metal bent back to form hooks. On the top hooks meat is hung, and on the lower ones, vegetables. The cone is set over a bed of coals, and as the meat roasts, the juices drip down, basting and flavoring the vegetables.

In Hong Kong I bought a set of Chinese cleavers, and at the central market in Valencia, a paella pan, which is somewhat like a giant two-handled frying pan for making that versatile rice-and-fish-or-fowl dish, so dear to Spanish hearts, and rapidly becoming Americanized.

I can't begin to list the things I have discovered at Dehillerin's, that Parisian paradise for cooking buffs, but they include omelet pans and a gigantic copper pot.

My wine cellar is largely the result of my travels through France's fabled and fabulous wine country with the late Sir Cedric Hardwicke.

We became friends during the filming of *The White Tower* in Chamonix. Not only did I learn much about my own craft from him—notably, economy of motion; he could express more by standing still than any other actor I have ever worked with—but he also widened my knowledge and appreciation of fine wines.

At his invitation, I joined him in a tour of the wine provinces, beginning with the famed Wine Road, from Dijon to Santenay, and crowning the experience with a visit to Somerset Maugham at Cap Ferrat.

I returned from this pilgrimage of wine, wit and wisdom eager to incorporate into my own modest cellar not only the wines, but the counsel I had gleaned.

Most rooms designed for service as wine cellars are too small, and not well located as to dryness and temperature. In the matter of size, most people tend to think in terms of the racks that hold a dozen bottles, which supposedly present no problem as to space. What they fail to take into consideration is that some wines must age three to four years before they are used, and while the aging process is going on, you must have room for current stock.

The average wine cellar should accommodate from ten to fifteen cases, and the temperature range should be from 50 to 65 degrees. Location, too, is an important factor, because dampness can penetrate the corks. Earth movement or vibration can be a danger also. One of New York's finest restaurants once had its wine cellar literally wiped out by spoilage caused by the vibration of the subway.

Far from being an expensive luxury, or status symbol, the wine cellar is a relatively inexpensive part of your house, if it is included in the original plans, as was the case with mine.

Most of the rocks I accumulate in my travels wind up in the atrium. A few go to the garden or patio, and especially significant or valuable acquisitions find a resting place in a glass case.

Considering the time variations of their points of origin, you might say I have rocks around the clock. I have picked them up in New Zealand, Switzerland, Austria, South Africa, Italy, France, England, Japan, Finland, Hong Kong, Hawaii and Washington, D.C. (the latter being represented by a brick from the White House, which I acquired at the time of the remodeling during President Truman's occupancy).

High point of the collection both literally and figuratively is the rock from the top of Mont Blanc. When I was in Switzerland making *The White Tower*, the *Syndicate des Guides* invited me to make the climb. The Swiss government requires you to have a physical examination before essaying the climb, and after you have made it, you understand the wisdom of the rule. I made the ascent in three days, and figure that I worked harder for that souvenir rock than for any other in the collection.

There have been occasions when my penchant for collecting rocks has landed me in difficulties. After I completed *The Green Glove*, in Paris, I decided to take the Orient Express to Vienna.

At that time the city was divided into American, British and Russian sectors. Determined to get a rock from the banks of the Danube, I left the Sacher Hotel and strolled down to the river, only to find that the banks had been neatly cemented. On the Russian side, however, there was a beachlike area where I figured I could be fairly sure of finding rocks.

The bridge was crowded with pedestrians, and I joined the push to the Russian side. Down by the water I began assessing the rock supply, which was pretty good. But that was as far as I got. The rest of my brief stay on the wrong side of the Danube was taken up with explaining to a Russian soldier who knew no English, why I was examining their rocks with such concentration.

Ultimately he decided that I was just another crazy American, with rocks in his head as well as in his hand.

Peter and I ran into a similar problem, American version, when we tried to get some souvenir rocks from the Copacabana's serpentine path that extends for miles along the crescent beach. We didn't exactly have a communication problem from a verbal standpoint, but it's not easy to explain to a security guard exactly why you are prying up rocks with a nail file and a pocketknife, at one o'clock in the morning.

On the whole, it was easier to get the rock from the top of Europe's highest mountain.

All in all, I have scores of mementoes, tangible and intangible, to mark my travels.

Every time I step into the garden, whip up an omelet in the kitchen, stroll around the atrium, or relax in the sauna, I have that round-the-world feeling.

20   Cabbages Is Beautiful

I am all for private enterprise. When it became obvious that the supply of vegetables at our place was going to exceed the demand, I began giving away the surplus. Peter took a larger view of the situation.

"What're you gonna charge for them?" he asked, as I set off with a grocery carton filled with fruits of toil and soil.

"Charge for them?" I exclaimed. "These are for friends. You don't charge your friends."

"How about strangers?" he asked. "How about if I have a vegetable stand, like those ones you're always telling about? I could make a lot of money!"

It seemed a harmless sort of business, and had the added value of teaching him some of the basics of finance. I thought it over, and finally gave my permission, along with a few words of caution: Don't overcharge. Don't high pressure the customers. And always say thank you.

Resourceful, enterprising, ambitious—it was a great satisfaction to see how the boy was developing.

I was almost sorry I was going out that afternoon to visit friends down at Portuguese Bend, which meant I would be leaving the house around three o'clock, just when traffic past the vegetable stand was picking up. On the other hand, I reflected, it might be better for Peter to be on his own.

I went out to see how the stand looked. He had found an old tile topped table that had been retired to the garage, and polished it up to its colorful best. It made an effective background for the wares displayed on it. In fact, my son was exhibiting considerable marketing know-how.

He had scrubbed the root vegetables until they were immaculate, and groomed the lettuce and cabbage to a cosmetic state worthy of a booth at the Farmers' Market.

A scene from Edna Ferber's *So Big* awoke in my memory. The young school teacher, Selina Peake, driving through the Illinois farmlands, exclaims as they pass a field of cabbage, "How beautiful it is here!" At which the stolid farmer beside her on the wagon snorts derisively, "Cabbages is beautiful?" But of course they are. All growing things are, and vegetables most of all—ask any artist.

"You ought to put up a sign," I suggested. "Some sort of eye-catcher. People don't often see vegetables and fruits as fancy as these."

"That's right," Peter agreed. He stared off into space for a moment, then left for regions of tackhammer and cardboard.

I went off with a sense of satisfaction and quiet pride.

When I got home that night, Peter was already in bed. There was no sign of his commercial enterprise out front, which pleased me again, since it showed a sense of order and responsibility.

I couldn't resist looking in on him, in the hope that he might still be awake.

He stirred and sat up, like any intelligent eight-year-old when you turn on the light.

"Gee! Sorry!" I said. "Did I wake you up?"

"It's okay," he said. "Did you have fun at the barbecue?"

"Fine, fine," I said. "But what I want to know is, how was business?"

"It was pretty good," he said offhandedly.

"How much did you take in?"

"Twenty-one eighty-three," he said promptly.

"Twen . . ." I stopped and stared. "Boy!" I switched off the light and tiptoed out. "Go to sleep," I said softly. "Tomorrow's another day."

At breakfast the next morning, I had a lot of father-type jokes ready, like, "It's great to know I've got you to fall back on, if the acting business ever goes sour." And "Maybe I ought to get them to make a place for you at the studio. If you can make carrots sell like that, think what you could do with corn!" This is the ha-ha type of humor I don't usually allow myself as a parent. Kids like to be taken seriously, and believe me this boy was dead serious about the fruit and vegetable business.

He didn't even bother to laugh politely. He said, "Gee, Dad, I gotta get my stand set up. M'I be excused?" He left in the middle of my best line.

21   Who's Minding the Store?

The next day was Saturday, and I looked forward to watching from a distance the drama of commerce at the front curb. To be honest, there are not many times when I regret being well known, but this was one of those occasions when it would have been pleasant to be less recognizable. I might even have gone out front and minded the store for the proprietor when he took a break.

About ten o'clock, just as I was starting out the door, the phone rang. It was a neighbor on the next block. "Say, Glenn," he began. "Uh, that's quite a boy you got there."

"You're not kidding," I agreed. "Do you know what he's doing? He's got a little stand, and. . . ."

"I know. I was there, yesterday," he said, a little self-consciously, it seemed to me.

"Do you know what he took in?" I inquired, with paternal pride.

He snorted. "I don't know what he took in, but I sure liked what he was giving out. You sure it's okay with you?"

"It's with my full approval," I confirmed.

There was a muffled sound from his end of the line. A feminine voice in the background said sharply, "*Tell* him, John!"

"Tell me what?"

"Listen, Glenn," he said, "do you really know what Peter's doing?"

"Certainly I do. He's selling homegrown vegetables."

There was one of those weighted silences. Then, "The hell he is!" said my neighbor. "Have you checked your wine cellar lately?"

I hung up the phone and stood there for a moment. "Wine cellar!" I started for that region on the run, stopping just outside the door. "I'll ask him," I muttered. "He wouldn't . . . but on the other hand. . . ."

Somebody brushed past me. "Excuse me," he said.

"*Wait a minute!*" I ordered. "I want to know. . . ."

"Please, Dad!" he said, "I gotta get back. Nobody's watching the store." He darted into the wine cellar. "I need another bottle of imported Coke."

I stood in the doorway, "dumbstruck," as my grandmother used to put it. He went unerringly to the space where only yesterday six bottles of Mouton Rothschild had reposed. There were four left.

I reached forward and removed the bottle from his hand. "Where do you think you're going with that?" I demanded. "Do you have any idea what that stuff's worth? That's my twenty-five dollar a bottle Mouton Rothschild. And where are the other bottles?"

"I sold 'em," he said. "Gee," he added, "you said it was

just imported Coke. Besides I only sell 'em to people that buy more'n a dollar's worth of vegetables."

Imported Coke. My Mouton Rothschild. It was true, I had in a moment of flippancy, when Peter asked what was in the bottles, said it was "imported Coke."

We went swiftly and silently out to the curb. The stand was not, after all, unwatched. It was under the delighted surveillance of five tourists. They were taking pictures of each other, with the stand and the house as background.

"Move over, Ethel," the man with the camera was saying, "you're blotting out the house."

There were some kindly guffaws from the others, with happy comments on the subject of Ethel's girth—the merriment not being shared by Ethel.

Peter had followed my advice about an eye-catching sign. It was large, and so was the printing. It began with VEG at the top, but the letters had been crossed out, indicating a lost battle with orthography, and replaced with FRUTES FROM MOVIE STAR GLENN FORDS GARDON. 25 CENTS EACH.

In slightly smaller lettering below, as befitted one taught the virtues of modesty and humility, was the legend: PICKED BY PETER FORD, SON OF GLENN FORD, STAR OF MOVIE PICTURES.

"Hey, kid!" called the camera man, "how about that imported French Coke?"

"We ran out," said the purveyor of Mouton Rothschild gloomily.

But they weren't listening.

"Say! There's Glenn Ford!" yelled Ethel. "Listen, Mr. Ford, I've seen every picture you ever made—clear back to *Heaven With a Barbed Wire Fence!*"

Why is it, they never remember the blockbusters?

22   Fly Swatter, Anyone?

If bugs could read, about all we would have to do to keep them under control would be to post the insecticide labels in appropriate spots, and they would all drop dead of fright.

As a matter of fact, it can be something of a shock to a moderately sensitive human to read some of the labels.

I don't mind admitting that I have never developed a cavalier attitude toward chemicals for garden or house. I do not use chemical fertilizers or sprays; I believe that a certain amount of the chemical, even though not in lethal doses, is inevitably going to be absorbed by the fruit, and affect its flavor, and possibly you.

Anyway, I can't see any reason for inflicting chemicals on a harmless plant that can't help itself. If it could, it would probably yank itself up by the roots and hurl itself over the fence, convinced that floricide was preferable to insecticide.

Additionally, I have a theory that seems to be a workable one, that if the soil is clean, free of infection, and balanced correctly for the plants concerned, you won't need insecticides.

I am a label reader. I don't read just the directions on the upper part—I go on down to the very bottom, to the print that says in letters $\frac{1}{64}$th of an inch high, "Harmful if swallowed, inhaled or absorbed through the skin . . . Do not spray on humans, pets, water, plants, food stuffs or utensils."

By the time you have checked to see that none of those items referred to are around, the wireworms have died of old age, and the flies are in the house, instead of outside in the patio.

Let's say, however, that you go ahead, grit your teeth and use the stuff anyway (being careful to observe all indicated precautions). You're still not home free. Your troubles are just beginning.

DO NOT ALLOW PETS OR CHILDREN TO CONTACT TREATED SURFACES UNTIL DRY.

I take this to mean until the spray dries, although the sentence structure might understandably give rise to concern about children or pets who might be wandering around, fresh from pool or tub.

I would like to meet the fellow who writes those labels. He's probably a first cousin to the one who wrote on the subject of drying sunflower seeds, PICK HEADS WHEN DRY AND HANG UPSIDE DOWN IN A DRY PLACE. Who, me?

Or the one who wrote the directions for eradicating the cutworm menace from tomatoes: PUT ON A PAPER COLLAR WHILE TRANSPLANTING. Gloves I can understand, but—a paper collar?

Fish emulsion, which seemed to me a nice substitute for the old Indian custom of tossing ripe minnows into the corn rows, describes itself as "an organic plant food derived from concentrated fish solubles." That sounds good, until you get to the part that says: CAUTION! CONTAINS PHOSPHORIC ACID. AVOID CONTACT WITH EYES OR CLOTHING. AVOID PROLONGED SKIN EXPOSURE. ANY SPILLAGE SHOULD BE IMMEDIATELY WASHED WITH WATER.

If it does that to people, what is it going to do to my corn?

Like Dickens' Rosa Dartle, I only ask because I want to know.

Even the snail pellet labels are enough to turn a strong man green. ATTRACTIVE TO CHICKENS AND DOGS. I'm safe there, anyway, thanks to the Beverly Hills police force and the Mason's cats. But it continues, HARMFUL DUST! AVOID CONTACT WITH SKIN, EYES AND CLOTHING. BURN OR BURY ANY EMPTY CONTAINER.

We are not allowed to have incinerators in Southern California, as it might lead to smog. So if passing neighbors should observe me or one of my household shoveling earth over something, it is just contaminated cartons. You don't like to throw anything that lethal in the trash cans. What if the trash collectors have a dog going along for the ride?

But it is the wording on the tomato powder that really impresses me. Evidently the manufacturers hire college professors or Philadelphia lawyers to write the labels.

BECAUSE CRITICAL, UNFORSEEABLE FACTORS BEYOND THE MANUFACTURER'S CONTROL PREVENT IT FROM ELIMINATING ALL RISKS IN CONNECTION WITH THE USE OF CHEMICALS, EVEN

100

THOUGH REASONABLY FIT FOR SUCH USE, BUYER AND USER
ACKNOWLEDGE AND ASSUME ALL RISKS. . . .

What bothers me is that "reasonably fit" stuff. It's ambiguous, is what it is. How fit is reasonably fit? To me, fit is one of those words with no degrees of meaning. It's fit, or it's unfit. A chemical powder of such lethal inclination is, it seems to me, no place for such semantic antics.

As for buyer and user "acknowledging and assuming all risks. . . ." I try to think back and recall whether or not anyone asked me at the time of purchase if I solemnly swore to assume "any and all risks in connection with . . ." etc.

I don't think they did. I think I would have remembered that one, and possibly checked with my lawyer before proceeding with the transaction.

That sort of assumption could lead to all sorts of complicated situations at the point of purchase, such as the presence and availability of notaries public, registration of buyers, forms in triplicate, and the like.

I'm not sure I could afford the risks involved, anyway, and I wouldn't feel easy, using the stuff without first going through a decontamination chamber before re-entering the atmosphere of my house.

The tomato powder classic adds, CAN BE USED ON BEANS UP TO WITHIN THREE DAYS OF HARVEST, ON POTATOES WITHIN ONE DAY.

Still, under the circumstances, I think the sporting thing is to have my dinner guests sign the simple legal form to the left of each plate, stating that they acknowledge and assume all risks for any food eaten on the premises.

101

Meanwhile, I am sticking with the tried and true method of dealing with any tomato worms that show up, which is to hand pick.

It is good to know that the fellows at the Pesticides Regulation Division of the U.S. Department of Agriculture are in there pitching for us.

They keep a watchful eye on those advertisers who tend to mix fact with fiction when describing the efficacy and safety of their products.

Some vaporizers, for example, highly touted as bug traps, have come under close scrutiny, and are not recommended for home use because of doubts concerning the safety of continuous exposure to the fumes.

Fly swatter, anyone?

23 Making the Earth Say Beans

My gardener is a master craftsman in all other aspects of gardening, but it has taken me six years to convince him of the folly of overwatering.

I don't water at all in the commonly accepted meaning of the term. I hand irrigate. Slow, easy, gentle. And I *never overwater*. Once a week is better than once a day.

In my opinion, irrigating or watering, whichever you want to call it, is one of the most undervalued and overlooked, of the gardening arts. Beginning gardeners especially, have a tendency to water all plants by the same standards. Yet the moisture requirements of the various plants vary considerably. You have to know your onions—and your carrots, tomatoes, banana squash, kale, cabbage and turnips, as well.

After all, we make all sorts of kindly inquiries of houseguests who may be with us no longer than a weekend, if we're lucky. What do they like for breakfast? How do they

103

like their eggs? Do they like to sleep in, or are they early risers? Breakfast in bed? Why didn't they stay home in East Pittsboro?

But in gardening, we bring in this helpless plant or seed, anchor him firmly in the earth, which may or may not be to his liking, then, every day, hot or cold, like it or not—*splat!* right in the face with the hose.

That's not irrigation—it's irritation. As far as I'm concerned, the only place for overhead sprinklers is in the shower or the atrium. Or on the lawn.

But then I don't fool around with lawns. They seem to me a great waste of time, space and labor. "Making the earth say beans instead of grass—this was my daily work," said Thoreau.

Making it say beans, onions, strawberries, tomatoes and carrots, instead of grass, seems to me even better.

Now obviously I can't do all my own watering, but I can determine just what is the best system to use with the particular crops and my methods of raising them, and let my gardener follow through.

I don't pretend to be an expert. I am merely setting down the procedures that have worked for me in my efforts to make the earth say other things than grass.

It is impossible to lay down hard and fast rules for watering because of differences in climate conditions, soil structure and other factors. I can speak only from my own experience.

I use a wand for watering. This is a long, slim aluminum hose attachment—actually an elongated nozzle, about four feet in length. It puts the water where it's needed, which is at the base of the plant.

In addition to the wand, a canvas hose soaker is an effec-

104

tive way to irrigate, since it allows the water to feed out slowly enough so that it does not run off before it can soak into the soil, or wash topsoil away. At the price of topsoil, you get so you take these things into consideration.

It's as important to know your soil as to know your plants. Remember that the sandy soils absorb water faster than, for example, hard, clay soil; also that beds with poor drainage can retain the water to the extent that roots will rot. And keep in mind that *plants can drown*. Learn the individual water requirements of each crop. Know your soil, and let this knowledge govern your irrigation habits. Have a heart—your plants can't yell *help!*

If you like window boxes, those wonderful minigardens, but dislike the chore of watering them, here is a good system. Get a quantity of quarter inch copper tubing (you can usually find it at any Army Surplus store), and run it from the spigot up to the boxes. It is flexible, thus it is easily maneuverable. Perforate the tubing at one-inch intervals along the section that is to lie in the boxes. Then, by a twist of the faucet, you have an automatic watering system.

This is especially practical for second story boxes, because it is relatively simple to run the copper tubing up the side of the house.

If you utilize every square foot of space (which I do) remember to plant water-loving plants together, and the same with shade and sun-loving plants.

If you use mulch to conserve moisture, keep it loose at the base of the plants; otherwise it packs down hard and defeats its purpose. It's surprising how many beginning gardeners assume that mulch is going to nourish the plants—that it somehow replaces fertilizer or plant food, whereas it is merely nature's thermal blanket, keeping the roots warm in winter and cool and moist in summer.

Another reason to eschew overhead watering is that it overwets the foliage, which leaves it susceptible to plant diseases. Also, hard watering splashes earth on leaves and fruit.

I spread a layer of straw no more than an inch deep in the beds of such plants as strawberries, eggplant, melons, squash and cucumbers—any plants whose fruit lies on the ground. Spread the straw when the plants are just up. Chopping it makes for easier handling and spreading, and it will lie flatter especially under the smaller fruits.

This serves several purposes: it keeps the fruit clean, prevents the ground from baking or washing, and it also serves as a weed deterrent. I consider its value a surface matter only, although some gardeners recommend spading it under in spring to add organic matter to the soil as the straw decays.

24   Snacktime in the Garden

I have occasionally been misunderstood when suggesting to my guests that they go outside and throw their butts into the rose bed. I refer of course to cigar butts. Wonderful fare for roses.

It's strange that we are always thinking of ways to vary our own diets, forever devising new methods of preparing and serving food, and going out of our way to get the latest and best in pet foods, yet we often overlook the fact that plants, too, like a treat now and then.

Compost, of course, is the garden smorgasbord, but there are additional appetizers that will give your plants a lift, and take the drudgery out of being a Brussels sprout or an artichoke.

Leaf mold, for one, is a tasty morsel, but if it isn't practical to hie yourself out to the woods to shovel this valuable commodity into gunny sacks (even supposing you could locate any woods), you might try some simple home touches like

107

coffee grounds, which because of their acid content, are a favorite hors d'oeuvre of azaleas and rhododendrons.

Corncobs, I have been told, are liked by roses as well as by most varieties of vegetables. One expert suggests having your farmer-neighbor grind some extra cobs for you, but I have run into a little difficulty along those lines. There seems to be a great dearth of corn and farmer-neighbors in Beverly Hills.

Wood ashes make a tasty snack, but don't go offering them to your azalea, camellia or rhododendron friends—or to potatoes, either, because of their lime content. Use them practically anywhere else, but don't combine them with manure. Wood ashes are excellent sources of potash and lime and phosphorus. Their main value is to give strength and resilience, and to develop strong stems.

Coal soot is often recommended because it repels snails, wireworms and cutworms. Unfortunately, it also repels me.

I have five chimneys, which would insure an adequate supply of soot for my garden, except for the fact that I prefer wood fires to coal. Anyway, the procedure of transferring soot from chimney to garden is naturally a complicated one.

My grandmother used to tell of the chimney sweeps of her girlhood, in London, when the small urchins employed by the chimney cleaning contractors would race each other up the sooty course, and emerge, shouting "Raw! Raw!" and waving their brushes.

I don't know whether the cry of "Raw! Raw!" was chimney sweep jargon for "Hurrah!" or "Raw deal!" which it certainly was, considering the shape they were in when they reached the top.

I collect old advertising cards—those colorful pasteboards

our grandparents delighted to add to the pages of scrap-books, and by which Pear's Soap, Ayer's Sarsaparilla, and others caught the public eye and purse. My collection under a glass top almost covers the surface of a big coffee table in my den. One, with the legend, COMPLIMENTS OF THE SEASON, though it doesn't have the advertiser's name, was indubitably a soap advertisement. It presents two sooty mites shaking hands across the chimneys, while angels beam down approvingly. Chimney Christmas!

That reminds me—never use coal ashes in your compost, only wood ashes.

Many people consider straw a tasty snack for the garden, especially when combined with leaves and laid on top of the soil to be left throughout the winter to protect against washing during heavy rains. Chopped straw is recommended as a mulch for raspberries and strawberries.

This brings up problems such as the necessity of adding nitrogen to counterbalance the high carbohydrate content of the straw mulch. In my opinion, the benefits are not that high (as I have mentioned before: I use the straw primarily to keep the fruit clean), and the whole business becomes a matter of mulch ado about nothing.

As far as compost heaps are concerned, turning over a new leaf is not nearly as important as turning over an old one.

The word compost means "a mixture or composition," and the ingredients for this garden smorgasbord can be endlessly varied.

Mine is composed—or decomposed—of leaves, some surface soil, such kitchen scraps as carrot tops, turnip and potato peelings, a little kelp, manure and chopped straw.

Mix well, moisten, and toss every three months or so.

The important thing about a compost heap is to keep it turned, loosening the materials with a spading fork occasionally. "Turning" doesn't mean heaving the whole mess up and over like a tossed salad, but lifting and more or less fluffing it, to enable air to circulate.

I don't add chemicals to my compost, but I add a little manure to insure the nitrogen content.

Like everything else these days, compost can get extremely complicated. There is a fairly new system—or new to me—of covering the pile with a plastic drop cloth such as you get at paint stores. This makes it unnecessary—also impossible—to turn or lift the heap. But on the other hand, you can't use it until something like eight months have passed, when it is presumed to be done, and ready for serving to various hungry mouths around the garden. I prefer having "ready to go" compost dinners.

While, as I mentioned before, cigar butts are good for your roses, that's about the only helpful thing about tobacco where the garden is concerned.

If you have friends who are addicted to the twin compulsions of smoking and fruit squeezing, watch out. All of us are familiar, most of us at first hand, with the squeeze play we feel compelled to make when we see a ripe peach or a tomato at its blushing best. PLEASE DON'T PINCH OUR FRUIT implores a sign on a Farmers' Market fruit stand. KEEP YOUR HOT LITTLE HANDS OFF OUR BERRIES, says another. Every home gardener should have similar warnings posted about the grounds.

This pinch, press and squeeze syndrome is understandably

the bane of market people. It is closely related to the tire-kicking syndrome, and just about as meaningful.

Beware, when you are conducting friends who smoke through the pleasant by-ways of your garden. Keep an especially keen eye on them as you approach the regions of tomatoes, red or green peppers, eggplant and petunias (I'm coming to that further on).

If you see your visitors bending forward in the time-honored pose of the fruit squeezer, knock them briskly to one side, and then laughing lightly to show that you know the whole thing sounds ridiculous, and that you are not some kind of a nut, suggest that they go into the house and wash their hands with soap and water, before touching the fruit —if they *must* touch it.

You may lose a few sensitive friends this way, but you'll be doing the eggplants, tomatoes, peppers and petunias a real favor.

Tobacco mosaic is a high-sounding disease that attacks these plants if they are handled by smokers with traces of nicotine on their hands.

It occurs to me that this information could spark a whole new campaign in the present concerted effort to discourage smoking. I hereby pass it along to the campaigners, free of any restrictions, and with absolutely no rights reserved.

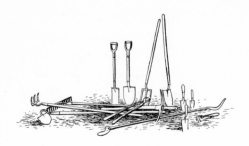

25　One Touch of Nature

When I began to get really serious about gardening, I thought of it as a simple, close-to-nature pursuit, in which a man could get to know the earth and, by a reasonable amount of grubbing in it, arise refreshed and enriched in body and spirit.

I viewed the whole thing with the happy, idealistic outlook Shakespeare expressed when he observed that "One touch of nature makes the whole world kin."

I don't recall, in my sparse delving into the matter of the bard's background, that he was much of a husbandman. If he was, he might have noted that one touch of nature also tends to make the back stiff and the muscles painful.

And in his day, they didn't even have available (at considerable expense) the complicated, lethal looking weaponry disguised as garden implements, which we have confronting us on every trip to hardware store or nursery.

There is a thing called a stand-up model grass trimmer that guarantees to do away with calloused knees and aching backs, through the benefit of three position swivel-cutting head sets. This is primarily for trimming and edging. There is also available a long-reach pruner that looks a little bit like an ostrich in the throes of hiccups.

I bought the things. However, I was never able to understand the directions, and my gardener refused to get involved with them at all. I finally returned them to the nurseryman who commented sadly that "they don't make things like they used to," but my complaint was that they don't explain things like they used to.

I went back to the basic tools like hoes, rakes, trowels, spading forks, pruning shears and pickaxes.

I had expected to do a good deal of leaning on the handle of a spade and staring into the heart of a rose, having been led to believe by everyone from Shakespeare to Thoreau, that a considerable amount of that sort of thing went on among gardening buffs.

What I wound up doing mostly was leaning on the handle of a spade and staring into the hostile eyes of wireworms and cucumber beetles.

That was in the early days of the project. The happy time of mulling over books about how to go about it. RAISE YOUR OWN MEALS! BEAT THE HIGH COST OF LIVING! MAKE A BOWER OF YOUR BACKYARD!

No mention was made of obstacles to be overcome: of the hazards of stubborn soil, sore muscles and dedicated insects.

Where did Thoreau get time to think those long leisurely thoughts? Obviously he didn't have to make a living at anything else while he was cultivating beans. According to him, his only enemies were worms, cool days, and woodchucks.

What I began gradually to become was less of a Thoreau man and more of a Charles Dudley Warner exponent.

"What a man needs in gardening," said Mr. Warner, "is a cast-iron back, with a hinge in it."

26 It Helps to Have a Sense of Humus

Gradually I was coming to the conclusion that what was wrong with the remaining original soil was a lack of humus. The garden columns and books kept referring to the need for "fertile soil material, rich in humus."

"With a sufficient amount of humus . . ." they would begin ponderously, and maunder on about the magnificent crops you would then be able to grow. "Your grass will have enough humus from roots and clippings . . ." they would say casually.

But they never said what humus was.

They seemed to take it for granted that they were talking to people who knew these things already.

A friend of mine tells of being assigned at the beginning of World War II to the same writer's pool in the Army Signal

Corps with another writer who subsequently attained fame and fortune in the world of letters.

Faced with an assignment to turn out a script for a Transportation Corps training film on "How to Load a Boxcar," that prolific and erudite author who was not one to suffer fools gladly, approached the subject with characteristic forcefulness.

At the appointed time he turned in a manuscript some thirty pages thick. On the cover was the title: *How to Load a Boxcar*. On the first page, "Transportation Corps, U.S. Army."

The next page, which was followed by twenty-seven others, all blank, read with classic simplicity:

Any damn fool knows how to load a boxcar.

Sometimes I get the feeling that gardening books have the same attitude toward humus. The prevailing opinion is, apparently, that any damn fool knows what humus is.

I didn't.

One day I thought it was finally going to be revealed to me when I came across a sentence beginning "Soils that are rich in humus . . . ," but the parenthetical description was merely "the stable product of decomposed organic matter."

Was I any better off than before? What kind of stable did they mean? Stable, as in a building for beasts to lodge in? (Webster.) Stable, as in steadfast, firm, fixed? (Webster again.) Stable as in horse manure? (Western movies.)

With all those definitions of "stable," Webster was surprisingly uncommunicative about "humus," describing it as

116

"a brown or black material formed by the partial decomposition of vegetable or animal matter; the organic portion of soil."

I went out and looked at the soil. The whole mess looked fairly organic to me. I still didn't know what humus was.

In the brief period of twenty-four hours or so when I had been rooting around in the mysteries of alfalfa, I had encountered the term COVER CROP and eventually learned that the magic words, GREEN MANURE, which had so baffled and intrigued me, pertained to any crop which is plowed under in fall or spring in order to add, through its roots and tops, humus to the soil. But I *still* didn't know what they meant by humus.

Why is there never a section in gardening books headed simply and openly, HUMUS?

I have never found it treated frankly and basically for the beginning tiller of the soil. This is not to say that it isn't waiting somewhere in some erudite tome, eager to reveal its mysteries to the baffled beginning gardener. But I have never come across it.

Was it something you could buy, like topsoil? Could you pick up the phone and casually order a hundred pound sack of the stuff? Somehow I thought not. I thought not so strongly that I couldn't bring myself to ask.

Then, one day I discovered—I forget where, in a gardening column, book or encyclopedia—that humus is "decomposed organic matter." There it was—I knew what it was made of, even if I didn't know what it was.

Stealthily I began backtracking. Back to the gardening column with its reference to humus as the "stable" product of decomposed organic matter. Back to the dictionary with

117

its claim that humus was "material formed by the partial decomposition of vegetable or animal matter." Back to the book that called it a "jelly-like substance derived from organic sources. . . ."

I threw them all together, shook them down, and what emerged was Ford's definition of humus for the beginning or non-humus-oriented gardener:

Humus is a substance derived from decomposed or decomposing vegetable or animal matter in the soil.

I had cracked the code!

I knew!

That's why we have compost heaps; that's why we plant cover crops; that's why we can thank every mole and mouse and gopher that meets its end beneath the ground, and every earthworm that eats and digests and excretes. They are all creating humus, just for us. That's why grass cuttings and coffee grounds, turnip peelings and carrot tops, and falling leaves, may be a nuisance to the nongardener, but are riches to the gardener.

The whole confusing experience left me with one question shouting silently from my battered soul: Why isn't there a Gardener's Dictionary? Illustrated.

I don't mean one of those tomes filled with terminology any child can understand. That blows it, right there. I am not prepared to cope with the words today's child can understand.

At a friend's house the other day I watched a brisk Ping-Pong match between the host and his nine-year-old son, which included a discourse on the aerodynamics of Ping-

118

Pong balls. Words like thrust, drive, air resistance and stress whizzed through the air faster than the balls.

The boy explained it all casually and expertly, while winning five out of six games.

No, what I am looking for is a Simple Gardener's Dictionary for the Simple Gardener—written, in short, for people just like me.

27 And Cast of Thousands

Gardening is the world's greatest variety act. It is comparable to a mammoth production with a cast of thousands—stars, extras, bit players—all with their special talents and roles to play.

Of course, like good talent of any kind, they need good direction to bring out their potential.

The theatre, or garden area, may be small, and therefore limited as to cast and programming; or it may be a sprawling and elaborate amphitheatre, fitted out for spectacular productions. They are equally challenging.

You, the gardener, are of course the combination producer-director-talent scout.

What makes the whole production endlessly rewarding is the fact that you are constantly discovering new talents among your cast, and devising effective and spectacular ways to highlight them.

You will find yourself having to deal with scene-stealers

and overly competitive performers that will have a tendency to dominate the stage.

Of course, if you are a clever entrepreneur, you have planned your production carefully, so that the performers are happy, and the sets designed to show off their talent to the highest degree.

Take that sister act, the Peach Trees. They are among the most cooperative members of the cast, although like all artists, they have their little idiosyncracies—they hate wet feet. So be sure they have well-drained soil. It doesn't have to be the richest—it can even be heavy or sandy, just so it is not of a type or location to keep them standing in dampness.

One of their special talents (which many people tend to overlook when planting peach trees) is the decorative use for the blossoms. You don't have to be clever at flower arranging to make the best use of these petal-laden branches. They are endlessly versatile for table decorations, or in tall vases on the floor.

One of my peach trees has a specialty act; the New Zealand Saucer Peach gets its name from its shape. It is a rather flat fruit and for that reason is very effective served whole, or sliced across, and with a little peach brandy or Cointreau poured over it.

It was Edith Piaf who taught me to eat peaches with Champagne. *Pêche Piaf* is merely half a peach in a glass of the bubbly. The saucer peaches are excellent this way, too.

Later on, I have my fill of peach preserves, cobbler and sherbet, the latter being a specialty of my cook.

Thus my peach trees serve a dual purpose—a visual as well as a culinary feast.

Speaking of sherbet, brings to mind another member of

the garden cast, the Japanese persimmon. Pick these when they are soft to the touch, and place in the freezer until they are just firm enough to slice. Serve them as they begin to thaw. The taste and texture are remarkably like sherbet, and the flavor of course cannot be duplicated in ice cream or sherbet.

Oranges belong to the royal family of the garden theatre, in my opinion. Their members and talents are almost uncountable.

Here are a few of the orange specialty acts:

Grate the rind, and sprinkle it in pancake batter.

Baste roasting chicken with orange juice.

Add orange rind to string beans as they cook.

Add grated rind to baked beans.

Dry the rind in small pieces, and add to hot tea as it brews.

Sprinkle the juice on codfish balls. and also on pork chops just before serving.

If you like to start the day with lemon juice in hot water, try substituting orange juice. Much more palatable, and just as good a source of vitamin C and citric acid.

In fact, most recipes which call for lemon juice are quite as effective when the juice of the sourer varieties of orange is substituted.

Onions are the comedians and character actors of the garden variety show, and the only ones who need not worry

122

about showing their age. In fact, those oddly pretty blossoms which are onions gone to seed, are amazingly versatile as garnishes and seasonings.

I use the little individual seeds in salads (first, pinch off the tiny stem ends). They are particularly good in coleslaw, and add a pleasant nip to dips and sandwich mixes.

There is some argument about the practice of "rolling down" onion tops after the seeds appear, but I find it a good procedure. When the stalks are about two feet high, and have blossomed, grasp them firmly about midway of the stems, and bend them down to the ground. Bend, don't crush.

This stops the growth of the seeds, and all the strength then goes into the underground, or behind-the-scenes production.

Incidentally, if you place onions in the freezer half an hour or so before slicing, their performance won't bring tears to your eyes.

Strawberries have so many acts that they could have their own show. Considering the fact that there are around six hundred varieties, you can see that the possibilities are endless.

For a change from the stock performances such as shortcake, pie, or dipping the berries in powdered sugar, try this: mash sugared strawberries with a little water, put in ice trays and freeze.

They taste very much like strawberry sherbet when served in this fashion, and are much simpler to prepare.

Avocados are a versatile bunch, too. Try dicing them and adding to eggs just before scrambling.

No one should ever plant an avocado tree without planting a lime, at the same time. Then you have your best combination, with no more effort than it takes to reach up and pluck them. Lime juice sprinkled on avocado, and served on the half shell, is to me, the best way to serve them.

Of course, lemons are good stand-ins for limes and are as versatile as oranges, since in many cases oranges and lemons are interchangeable. I like to put a few drops of lemon juice on calves liver as it cooks, and sprinkle it on frying sausages.

For a variety act, try this when barbecuing: in a piece of heavy duty aluminum foil, put sliced carrots, celery, green peppers, a sprinkling of dill weed, about ¼ cup of salad oil, 2 teaspoons of salt, ¼ teaspoon of black pepper (fresh ground, always). Sprinkle over the mixture three tablespoons of brown sugar. Seal the foil, and place on the grill.

I try to have every variety of tomato available, from the little Red Cherry to the big Beefsteak. Rather than staking each plant, I support them with a "fence" of heavy twine strung between redwood stakes.

"Never give a sucker an even break" when dealing with tomatoes. Keep pinching off the little suckers or shoots that appear in the joint where the leaf and main stem join.

If you stagger your planting by starting as early as February (if you live where the frost danger is past by then) and plant the midseason and late tomatoes as the spring comes on, you always have another group of performers waiting in the wings.

Carrots and radishes are great encore artists too.

I am especially fond of fried tomatoes. Pick them while they are still a little green, slice and sprinkle with brown sugar, and fry. Or dredge in flour with plenty of seasoning, fry two slices of bacon for each tomato (this of course varies according to preference), and then fry the tomatoes in the

124

bacon fat. Make a cream gravy, pour it over the tomato slices, garnish with the bacon, and serve with hot biscuits.

Being able to pick the vine-ripened fruit is one of the great pleasures of having your own fruit and vegetable garden. Naturally it is economically impossible for commercial growers to let the fruit stay on vine or tree until it is eating-ripe, but it accounts for the lack of flavor in much of today's produce.

I grow cucumbers primarily for pickling, but they are equally as tasty served fresh with sour cream. If they are young and tender enough, leave the peel on, scoring with the tines of a fork before slicing.

Actors learn early that corn is good only when fresh, and this is true also of garden corn. Use it as soon as possible after picking. I like to smear corn on the cob with sour cream, wrap it in foil and roast.

Usually in planning the garden extravaganza, I include a few pumpkin vines. They are colorful and traditional decorations at Thanksgiving, and of course great for Halloween jack-o'-lanterns. I generally plant Connecticut Field Pumpkins, or Big Max, which reach a tremendous size. They are a traveling act, however, and will need roughly fifteen square feet of space to ramble over.

I have heard it said that you should never mix certain vegetables, since they have a tendency to trade flavors. I think it might be interesting if they did. Onion-flavored watermelon, or cucumbers that taste like concord grapes might be a gastronomic sensation.

I have my onions growing next to cucumbers and grapes, however, and so far they have never tried to upstage each other.

125

28   Bare Roof Oranges

I returned from viewing the gardens of Versailles with the idea of an orangery tucked away in the suitcase of my mind.

It should be said at once that my method of developing space for an orangery is not likely to be widely copied. For one thing, very few people plant every inch of arable space, as I seem to have done, and therefore the problem would not arise. If it did, hardly anyone would feel that the end justified the extremely complicated means by which I acquired the needed space.

It all came about, as I have said, because I had been inspired by the beauties of the gardens at Versailles, and in particular by the orangery, so that I came home filled with dreams of trees laden with golden globes of fruit, standing in some sun-drenched portion of my garden not as yet revealed.

It wasn't revealed because it wasn't there—the space, that is. I studied the terrain and realized that the only unplanted area was in the paths between the beds. Very well then, having used up all the space on the ground, I would proceed to the roof.

From the beginning, I was positive that this was not a project I could broach with any amount of confidence, to my business manager. I knew it would never pass the Is It Deductible? test. In his book, and all too rightly, the height of folly would be exactly the distance between roof garden and ground.

My house, having a flat roof, seemed the ideal spot for a roof garden, but on the other hand, this would necessitate some sort of outside stairway. The guest house, however, is at the foot of the driveway, some distance below the level of the main house. Unfortunately, it had a peaked, tile roof.

I was once a guest at a "topping out" ceremony and had been intrigued by the hoisting of a symbolic young tree up to the top of the skyscraper to celebrate the completion of the highest story. In houses, the ceremony is used when the rooftree or ridgepole is set in place.

Why, I wondered, shouldn't I reverse the procedure? I would take the roof off, and hoist up several dozen trees instead of one. Once the peaked roof was removed from the guest house, the flat top would be almost on a level with the garden area immediately behind it.

As I mentioned, this is not recommended procedure.

There is no point in going through the complicated construction and destruction problems of lowering a roof in order to raise a garden. I could never explain it in technical terms. I drew up my plans, turned them over to the architect and took off for Spain to make a picture. I thought it would be just as well to be out of town when the bills reached my business manager's desk.

When I returned, my guest house had a flat roof which had been so ingeniously joined with the land behind it that I could hardly tell where the roof left off and the ground began.

The surface was covered with white gravel, to reflect heat and light, and in redwood tubs, the first of the trees I had ordered, stood around awkwardly like strangers at a reception, waiting to be introduced.

The question has often been raised—and with particular earnestness by guests invited to spend any time in the guest house, as to whether such an assortment of good-sized trees in tubs and pots would not put a severe strain on the roof supports.

I can tell them with complete assurance that a house that supported a full tile roof is not likely to groan under the weight of several dozen trees.

Water—both rain and irrigation—is not a problem either, because adequate drainage has been provided.

Watering of the trees is carefully controlled, because if there is one thing citrus trees dislike, it is a slosh of water standing around on their roots. They need well-drained fertile loam soil which should be allowed to dry out between watering. Too much water will make the roots begin to rot, and if the wet, soggy soil is allowed to lie against the trunk for long periods, any tree with an ounce of spunk will break out with Gummosis, an affliction which causes the bark to sweat large amber drops of gum.

I began with Meyer lemon, Rangpur lime, dwarf navels, both Robertson and Washington, and Kara mandarin. More

128

recently I have added Nagami kumquat, dwarf tangerines, Bearss lime and Temple orange. The latter, which the Chinese call Sweet Tree, is actually more shrub than tree.

Meyer lemon is a dwarf hybrid with fruit that is smaller and more acid than the standard lemon. It is especially well adapted to a garden like mine because it thrives in a pot and produces abundantly.

To me, the limes are the most interesting of the citrus fruits. My favorite is the Rangpur lime. "Lime green" is a misnomer here, since it is a bright orange, indicative of its derivation from lime and mandarin, which also explains its orange, red-tinged skin and fruit. It is more resistant to cold than are lemons and true limes (and we do have cold weather in Southern California occasionally).

Bearss lime is a seedless variety, more acid than the Rangpur, but even more flavorful. It has the traditional yellow-green skin, and is a rapid grower. Mine is doing well in an oversize redwood tub, but since this variety grows slightly larger than the other limes, it may be transplanted eventually to the ground level.

On the subject of the tubs, I have learned to do it myself, since most nursery tubs are eighteen inches square at their largest, and extremely expensive if you get into custom-made sizes. I use redwood, as I do with the planting beds, because it does not warp, shrink or rot.

One of the advantages of planting in tubs or pots is that you have a movable garden, and it is relatively simple to change the positions and locations of the trees as they increase in size. At first I place them from six to twelve feet apart, but this is adjusted according to the tree's development. One thing I would point out to the beginner, when

129

transplanting trees, try to duplicate the exposure—the side of the plant that faced south, for example, should be replanted in the same position.

Don't fail to remove the nursery tag on trees. If you don't, the wire will cut into the bark as the tree grows, and you may lose an entire branch. If you have a large number of trees and are not good at names, put an identifying name tag on the container.

It is important, when you are planting dwarf varieties, to leave the bud union well above the soil. There are technical reasons for this which, I confess, escape me. I only know it is the wise and proper procedure, and oddly enough, exactly the opposite of that used in planting the standard fruit tree.

I learned in France that the best way is to have your aisles or rows running north and south. This assures the maximum morning and afternoon sun.

The dwarf varieties of navels, Washington and Robertson, are relatively hardy, and produce for most of the year. I have a Valencia, also, which is the commonest California orange, great for juice, but not the most practical for a pot, since it grows quite large.

Oranges and lemons are particularly decorative, since the fruit can be left on the tree long after it matures, and picked as needed. Limes and mandarins on the other hand, will get overripe if they are not picked as soon as they mature.

Lemons and many varieties of limes and mandarins have blossoms, young fruit and mature fruit on their branches at the same time during a good part of the year, which makes them particularly valuable from a decorative standpoint.

Kara mandarin, which I acquired primarily because it is an excellent juice fruit for mixing (so strong that it may be diluted by one half) is doing well, although the fruit is not as large, I am told, as it is when grown in the hotter, interior valleys. It ripens between April and July.

I particularly like mandarins because they are easy to eat right from the tree, having the loose, dry skin that comes off easily, with no mess—which gives them their nickname of "kid glove orange."

Tangerines are the deeper colored, almost reddish mandarins. I have the Dancy, which gives a good yield in the winter months, very sweet, but small and full of seeds.

Don't overlook the kumquat when you plan your orangery. I have the Nagami, which has an oval fruit. These are good for preserving, and also can be eaten fresh from the tree, skin and all. This is a heavy bearer, and the fruit can be left on the tree for months after maturing. It is ideal for growing in tubs or pots, being what is called a "true dwarf," ranging from two to four feet when grown from trifoliate rootstock. This is perhaps the hardiest citrus tree, and grows well even in the Pacific Northwest.

"Rootstock" is another of those words like "humus" which the novice encounters with similar bafflement. It is the parent root on which a desired variety is budded or grafted. Trifoliate orange seedlings are widely used for dwarfing purposes.

The great advantage of dwarf fruit trees is that they are so well adapted to pot and tub planting, which means that they are ideal for a rooftop operation such as mine. The dwarfs are more expensive than the standard trees because of the more complicated propagation process. I am still learning the various methods, and am at this point content to leave the process to the nursery from which I buy my trees. However, if you have the time and the knack, this is a fas-

131

cinating and rewarding aspect of gardening. The dwarfing rootstock for citrus is the trifoliate orange.

What it all boils down to is that an orangery is really not an orangery at all, but a citrusry—at least where mine is concerned—a combination lemonry, orangery, limery and kumquatery.

If you have the right climatic conditions, plenty of sun (particularly where the dwarf varieties are concerned—at least four hours a day) shelter from winds, and well-drained soil, you can easily establish an orangery, on a large or small scale.

Remember Ford's system of the expanding garden—when you have planted all arable ground space, when the patio will not accommodate one more tub or pot—be of good cheer: there's always a roof!

29 Delicious! What Is It?

People who like to raise fruits and vegetables are usually hearty eaters, and like to cook as well. In other words, your heart's not in it if your stomach isn't.

Certainly my own interest in the preparation of food has grown proportionately with the experience of raising it.

One of the pleasures of having a large and constant supply of homegrown foods is experimenting with new dishes. Just because you can't find it in a cookbook doesn't mean there aren't new and better ways of cooking and serving.

As a general rule, men are better cooks than women because they are more adventurous, willing to take chances and more inclined to improvise.

Try new combinations. Only four out of twenty may turn out successfully, but you may discover a new taste treat in the process. Even so mild an experiment as sprinkling Nescafe over vanilla ice cream may intrigue sophisticated palates, if served with the proper air of mystery.

It's wise to know your audience before you tamper with old favorites or introduce new dishes. Don't make the mistake of gathering a group of people with well-known food prejudices or digestive idiosyncrasies to preview a gastronomic creation.

There they sit, munching away, all smiles and happy murmurings: "Mm! (swallow) . . . this is great! I don't know *when* (gulp) I've had anything that tasted as *delicious* . . . (smack). What *is* it?"

"It's curried squirrel"; or "hen's feet au gratin," you say. But not if you're smart.

Instead, give it a French name and change the subject instantly. Lie a little, if necessary. "Children and fools speak true," said a sixteenth century sage.

Better yet, give it a Hungarian name. (Have a few handy for these little moments.) Most people will be ashamed to ask how to spell it. If they persist, say it's your cook's recipe, and she gets violent if asked to give it out.

Actually, the safest thing to do in these cases is to say it's chicken. People will believe anything is chicken if it comes to dinner wearing a casserole.

It was Ed Buchanan who was under contract to Columbia when I was, who taught me to make venison meat loaf. Make it just as you do a regular meat loaf, except that you will need more milk to get it moist enough:

2 lbs. venison	1 onion, chopped
2 lbs. pork	2 eggs
1 medium can kidney beans, drained	½ cup mik, or more
	Salt, pepper

Almost any vegetable is good french fried. I particularly like string beans, which retain their crispness, but summer squash, zucchini and cauliflower all are delicious.

Try adding chunks of pineapple to banana squash. And add a dash of Cognac or sherry to potatoes as you mash them.

Most people tend to overlook the versatility of potatoes and carrots. I find so many ways to use carrots that I stagger the plantings in order to have standby crews for a good part of the year.

My mother is famous for her carrot pudding. Served with lemon sauce instead of the richer, heavier hard sauce, it is a light and satisfying substitute for the ponderous plum pudding which many people find too "much of a muchness" after a hearty Christmas dinner. Here is her recipe:

LEANNA FORD'S CARROT PUDDING

Combine:

1 cup chopped suet	1 tsp. soda
1 cup brown sugar	1 tsp. salt
1 cup grated potatoes	1 cup raisins
1 cup grated carrots	1 cup currants
1½ cups sifted flour	½ cup mixed peel

¼ cup molasses

Steam four hours in a bowl with cheese cloth tied firmly over the top.

I don't know why the potato has been relegated to a lowly status in the vegetable social scale, when it can perform in such varied and delightful ways.

It is the only vegetable, as far as I know, to be immortalized by a monument. In Germany's Neckar Valley a monument was erected long years ago, inscribed "To God and

Francis Drake, who brought to Europe for the everlasting benefit of the poor—the Potato."

Judy Garland taught me that one of the most soothing dishes for a queasy stomach is mashed potatoes. I took Judy to some of the finest restaurants, with menus as big as her heart, only to have her order mashed potatoes, topped with a poached egg!

When I was growing up, we usually had Shepherd's Pie once a week. This is a delicious way to serve potatoes and to utilize left over roast.

It is hard to give a recipe for this, because it is really a Leftover Casserole. Grind the remainder of your roast, add part of the gravy to moisten, onion, pepper and salt, if necessary. When placed in the casserole, it should fill it about half way.

Add fresh mashed potatoes topping the meat. Make a swirl pattern on top of the potatoes with a knife, and brush with egg yolk. Bake at 300 degrees about an hour.

You can make additions to canned or prepared foods that will give them a complete personality change.

To canned corned beef hash, add a half teaspoon of thyme, two teaspoons of brown sugar (or one teaspoon of brown sugar and one teaspoon of maple syrup), and a couple of tablespoons of chopped scallions. Mix lightly, and brown in a hot pan with a tablespoon of cooking oil.

Serve scallops raw, dipped in soy sauce. The taste is very similar to Japanese Sashimi or raw tuna.

Add sliced bananas to peanut butter sandwiches.

136

The secret of cooking chicken livers is to soak them overnight in milk.

I have one firm rule in cooking. Don't overdo it. We have a national tendency to overcook, overserve and overeat, which visitors from abroad sometimes find more appalling than appealing.

"The problem with American hospitality," Prince Philip once observed, "is not so much how to return it, as how to survive it!"

And speaking of survival, it's a good idea to test your food experiments ahead. If you are inclined to be overcautious, force yourself a little—we would still be eating our meat raw, if no one had been willing to experiment, back there in the cave.

Of course you must use a little discretion in your experiments. Don't try to be so far out that you fall off the culinary edge.

Blind dates with foods can be as disastrous as with people —and conversely, can turn out surprisingly well. But don't take that chance with your guests unless you are sure of their adaptability.

The old doggerel about peas has stayed with me ever since childhood days.

> I eat my peas with honey,
>   I've done it all my life.
> It makes the peas taste funny,
>   But it keeps them on the knife!

But it isn't sufficient to convince me to serve peas and honey together!

30　Thyme on My Hands

Some people collect herbs like others collect stamps or coins. I collect only the ones I like to use: rosemary, thyme, basil, dill, tarragon, sage, parsley, chives and rose geranium.

As a matter of fact, I thought the primary reason for growing herbs was for their culinary uses; but that's just one of the reasons, and not necessarily the main one. Herbs have such a romantic, medicinal and sinister history in their various ways, that many herb gardeners seem more concerned with their background than their foreground.

I don't know where the expression, "herbs and simples" came from, but certainly herbs are simple to raise. Most of them have modest requirements as to soil and nourishment, so much so that they labored under a handicap for years because a rumor got out that they actually preferred bad soil.

One of their most appealing aspects as garden dwellers is that they don't have the attraction for insect pests that their less aromatic companions have. Try chewing up a leaf of basil or thyme, and you will understand why they are relatively pest-free. Although, come to think of it, if anything would repel bugs with its strong taste, it should be the onion, yet it doesn't appear to bring tears to the eyes of onion maggots.

Some gardeners claim that herbs are so unattractive to insects that it is a good idea to plant them near vegetables. I don't know whether or not it is a workable theory. I planted basil next to cherry tomatoes, but only because they have similar soil requirements.

I grow my basil from seed, sowing about a foot apart. One or two plants give me an ample supply of the leaves. It is one of the most fragrant of herbs, and when it goes to seed, it is, I think, one of the most distinctive and decorative. It was the Greeks who gave it the name of basil, meaning king, which is why the French refer to it as *herbe royale*. Just why it was given that high-sounding name, I don't know. It is an extremely democratic king—gets around to the most commonplace dishes, and has more uses than any herb I have, with the possible exception of thyme. Try it with soups, stews, and lamb chops.

It used to be the custom for Italian swains to signify "object matrimony" by sticking a sprig of basil in their hair.

If all of the people who have stared down at my herb garden and sighed, "There's rosemary—that's for remembrance," were laid end to end, that might be the best thing to do with them. It seems to be the only memorable thing Ophelia said, and I think it's high time something more quotable about this herb was devised. By the way—legend says rosemary grows well, only in gardens of the righteous. (I like to make that little point whenever I can.)

139

At one time I included fennel among my herbs, but that was when I liked to experiment with bread-making; the seeds have a licoricelike flavor, and are a tasty addition to rolls and bread, and some people like it sprinkled on apple pie. I prefer the pure apple taste.

I never could figure out Edna St. Vincent Millay's reference in one of her poems to stealing breath from a stalk of fennel—unless it was connected with the belief in biblical times, that it was one of the sacred herbs with curative powers for numerous diseases.

At any rate, I needed the space it took, and so replaced it with other, more distinctive and useable herbs.

Chives, now—there's something I wouldn't want to be without. I'm an omelet fancier, and chives make omelets fancier. They don't care too much when you plant them, spring or fall, but they are a little fussier about their soil than some herbs.

I like them in salads and soups, as well as in omelets and scrambled eggs. I sprinkle them over poached eggs, and of course they are important additions to cheese dips.

Dill is so plentiful in Southern California that it can be seen growing in vacant lots, by which you may gather that it is easy to grow, if you give it plenty of sun. I grow it chiefly for pickling uses, and maybe because it is so undemanding —it can be sown on top of cultivated soil, or planted in rows, and obligingly reseeds itself, so that while it is not a perennial, you have as much benefit from it as though it were. It germinates in around six or seven days, and comes to maturity in six weeks.

(In case the need should arise, it is nice to know it is a legendary witch-deterrent.)

Another of its long-ago attributes was that it was a sedative (which is interesting only because the dictionary describes the seeds as "a stimulant").

Keep in mind as you start a herb garden, that herbs vary radically in height and growth habits. Dill grows tall, four to five feet. So does fennel, and gawky rosemary gets up to six feet. So plant them where they won't hide or overshadow the smaller plants.

Thyme, on the other hand, is a sprawler (keep this in mind, and plan for enough space when planting it). Most varieties (mine is the commoner, *thymus vulgaris*) have a tendency to get woody, so it is a good idea to divide the clumps every couple of years, and start new ones. An easier way is layering, which I prefer. Simply lay the long stem over into a shallow trench, and cover with soil.

For drying purposes, cut it just as budding starts. (If you wait until it blooms, you must fight the bees for it.)

Cookbooks, in my opinion, are often overcautious in their recommendations as to the quantity of herbs to use. They recommend a "pinch of thyme" or a "pinch of rosemary," meaning an infinitesimal amount. When I say a pinch, I mean a three-finger pinch. If you come across that confusing term, "a sprig of thyme" in a recipe, make it a half teaspoon.

As for making the best use of thyme, I like it in so many things, it is hard to cover them all. I like it especially in stews, soups, fish sauces, meat loaf and poultry dressing—all the usual uses. As a matter of fact, it is hard to think of many meats that don't improve with thyme.

Pliny the Elder even recommended it as a mattress stuffing, claiming that it would cure melancholy. (This was probably

141

the earliest recorded instance of sleeping on your own thyme.)

It is easy to understand why people get so enthusiastic about herb gardening. If I had the space, I would begin the slow, delightful toil of accumulating all the well-known and little known varieties—with one exception. Rue can cause severe skin irritation. Some people are more susceptible to rue poisoning than others, but I have never bothered to find out if I am one who should never handle it. It may or may not be the source of the expression "to rue it," but certainly it is what you will do if you develop the severe dermatitis it causes.

With so many varieties of herbs to choose from, they could easily fill my limited planting beds, so I am not likely to expand my collection. But there is something intriguing to me about the propagation of such a plant as coriander, for one, which has been around almost as long as man himself, going back in recorded history as far as 5,000 B.C.

Any way you look at it, it's nice to have your own mint. There was even a time when it was like money in the bank, to the extent that such herbs as mint, anise and rue were tithed.

"You tithe mint and rue and every herb," said Jesus to the Pharisees, rebuking them for being scrupulous in small matters, but not in the things of greater importance, such as love and justice.

My mint is planted to get more shade than sun, under an apricot tree, but aside from keeping it well watered, about all I worry about is keeping it from taking over.

I like it especially in mint sauce, to serve with lamb, in juleps and jellies, and a bruised leaf or two in tea. I like to use it fresh, and, like parsley, it keeps well in a jar in the refrigerator.

I prefer to dry mint and dill without recourse to the oven. Wash the sprigs, and hang them upside down in a dry place, pantry or closet. For dust-free purposes let them hang in a paper bag, the stems sticking up out of the top of the bag, which is closed around them with a rubber band.

People take it for granted that an actor identified with Western movies is bound to have sage in his garden.

"Where's the sagebrush?" they chortle.

If you want sage advice from this actor, don't confuse prairie sagebrush with herbal sage, unless you like the flavor of turpentine, which is a characteristic of the former.

Herbal sage (*salvia officinalis*) wouldn't last as long as it takes to cut 'em off at the pass, if it had to grow on the lone prairie. It likes well-drained soil, a moderate amount of water with plenty of sun.

I started mine from seed, and it will grow from cuttings, but the best system is to divide the clumps when the plant is two years old. I find one good-sized plant is plenty for my uses.

Sage tea was, in the old days, a specific for colds, and it was thought that the herb guaranteed long life. I've tried sage tea, and think there must be a better way.

> Better a life of comparative brevity,
> Than drinking sage tea to insure one's longevity.

Tarragon's last name is Vinegar to most of us, but this herb is a great addition to chicken, especially boiled chicken, which I always feel needs all the help it can get. It is good with any tomato dish, and I like to add a few fresh leaves to salads. Tarragon likes a sandy soil, with good drainage, and both sun and shade. Mine does well in a terraced planting box.

My vote for the most fragrant herb goes to rose geranium. This is so easy to grow from cuttings, that it is surprising to find how scarce it is at nurseries. They want a sandy soil and good drainage. Mine has both sun and shade. They are a great addition to apple jelly, as well as in tea. Use only a part of a leaf in hot tea; the flavor is strong and penetrating.

Parsley is pretty enough to use as a border plant. It is slow to germinate, and many gardeners recommend soaking the seeds in warm water a few hours or a day before planting, but I have never been in that much of a hurry. It likes a rich soil, and plenty of sun.

In addition to its talents for garnishing, it is a staple in *fines herbes*, which is a fancy way of saying finely chopped mixed herbs. Combine it with chives and chervil; with basil and chives; or with watercress, tarragon and chives.

If you haven't ever had Herb Butter, you have missed one of the tastiest reasons for growing herbs. Spread on French bread and heated, this is a savory companion to stews, soups and spaghetti, as well as countless other dishes.

HERB BUTTER

2 cubes butter
1½ tsps. lemon juice
1 tb. sherry
2 tbs. finely chopped
   fresh parsley

¼ tsp. oregano (crush
   the leaves)
¼ tsp. rosemary
¼ tsp. thyme

144

Blend and spread between the slices of French bread, and lightly on the tops and sides. Then roll in foil, leaving open at top to get the crust crisp. Place in moderate oven for 15 or 20 minutes. Serve hot, of course.

Nobody ever seems to discover new kinds of herbs, and I often wonder if there aren't some talented weeds waiting around to find their right role. Many of our herbs were originally considered weeds until some medicinal value was discovered to elevate them in life. And dill is still commonly called dill weed.

Toadflax, according to Webster, is a common Eurasian perennial herb of the figwort family, yet is considered a weed in the United States.

Which just goes to prove the truth of Emerson's observation that "A weed is merely a plant whose virtues have not yet been discovered!"

31 The Dangers of a Happy Childhood

Like most other children, Peter formed attachments to various animals and objects which, to the adult, have little appeal. A lizard who made his home in a corner of the patio was not just a harmless reptile, but Peter's own personal lizard. He was so personal that Peter had composed a poem about him:

> I have a little lizard,
> And he hasn't any gizzard,
> But he sure is a wizard
> At catching bugs.

"He hasn't any *gizzard!* Certainly he hasn't any gizzard," said Mrs. Kelly. "He's not a chicken."

"I guess she doesn't know about poetry," Peter confided

to me. "There isn't anything but gizzard and wizard that rhymes with lizard."

About all I knew of lizards was that they were indeed wizards when it came to catching insects, and that they were addicted to tearing off their tails and throwing them down in a tantrum—the lizard equivalent, I suppose, to throwing down the gauntlet.

Their most enchanting quality as far as Peter was concerned was the ability to shuck off their skins, and for a long time one of his cherished possessions was the perfect transparent skin left tidily between the screen and the sliding glass doors of the living room.

But some of his friends were imaginary. When he was five or six, he had a whole houseful of make-believe characters who lived mostly in the walls, communicating with us by raps and whistles, for which I served as transmitter.

They included a mysterious midget named Richard, Freddy the Frog, and a mouse named Melvin.

Maybe it is a mistake to indulge a child's tendency to daydream, and to encourage his imaginative qualities, but I don't think so.

If he is aware that fantasy is just that, even daydreaming can be productive. Perhaps to be able, as Thoreau did, to "hear beyond the range of sound," and "see beyond the range of sight" should not be despised in a world that tends to make a religion of realism, rather than the other way around.

When Peter was very small, he was fascinated by the swimming pool. One day I had it drained, and a friend of mine, who was a set designer at Columbia, came over and painted an octopus on the bottom.

When it was filled once more I brought Peter out, and

147

pointing down into the water, I said, "That's Oscar the Octopus down there. He lives in the pool, and he doesn't like little kids swimming around in his house unless their parents are with them."

The face on the octopus was grouchy enough to be convincing, and the tentacles seemed to wave in the water. Peter, who hadn't learned to swim yet, lost interest in the pool.

Some of my friends had dark prophecies about the possible harmful effects of such make-believe on a child in later life. They spoke soberly of the dangers of implanting a fear of water, creating a sort of psychic hydrophobia that might make him fearful of such pursuits as surfing and swimming.

I had Oscar painted out a year or so later, but I never detected in Peter any horror of water, beyond the normal antipathy to baths, common to most young males.

In my opinion, childhood make-believe companions are fine, as long as they remain incorporeal. It's when they start fleshing out that you get into trouble.

Take Melvin. One night Mrs. Kelly set a trap in the pantry. Early the next morning, Peter, on the prowl for a pre-breakfast snack, discovered the trap and its defunct victim.

His voice, never known for its lack of power and carrying ability, filled the entire house.

"She killed *Melvin!*" he roared.

It was a nasty way to be awakened from a sound sleep.

I raced out to the kitchen, colliding with Mrs. Kelly and the corpse.

After I had soothed her and quieted Peter down, I took him back into the bedroom to explain matters.

I assured him that the mouse in the trap was not Melvin at all, but some interloper. Melvin never came out of the walls, I reminded him. "Did you ever know him to come out?"

"No-o," he hadn't. "But that's because he's invisible," he added, his face lengthening again.

"Then if this was Melvin," I reasoned, "you couldn't see him!"

"Yes I could, too!" he insisted. "If he was dead, he wouldn't be invisible any more!"

I can't explain it, but that sounded reasonable to me. I had to go back and pick up the first argument.

"Melvin," I assured him, "wouldn't come out of the walls *at all*. This was some outsider, looking for crumbs. Melvin wouldn't be caught dead out of his wall!" (I backtracked rapidly.) "I mean he wouldn't come out where there were people. It isn't," I concluded desperately, "as though he was a *real live* mouse!" All in all, an unfortunate choice of words.

"There isn't any telling what lasting damage a thing like this can do to a child's psyche," my housekeeper said forebodingly.

Personally I believe the psyche of a child raised with love, understanding and discipline is a lot more durable than people think.

What was really bothering her was the fact that Peter was crying. Like many women, she subscribed to the theory that tears in a male over four years of age were unmanly.

I don't go along with that. I have seen strong men cry, without any diminution of their masculine image. Eisenhower wept at the tribute paid Admiral Halsey, and Omar Bradley cried openly at Ike's funeral. I see no disgrace in tears compelled by deeply felt emotion. I have no patience with tears of rage or frustration, but I see no weakness in those "tears from the depth of some divine despair," which at one time or another most of us have, or will, shed.

I have not been ashamed of the emotions of grief or pity which have occasioned my tears, the few times in my adult life when I have wept, nor would I see them as manifestations of weakness in my son.

When we are too inured to cruelty to be torn by the evidences of it—too hardened by sights of devastation or degradation, spiritual as well as physical, to yield to tears—*then*, it seems to me, we are in danger of being unmanly.

But when we become so unemotional that the only thing that matters is to know that nothing matters, we have lost the thing that differentiates us from the animal.

"Heaven knows we need never be ashamed of our tears," wrote Dickens in *Great Expectations*, "for they are rain upon the blinding dust of earth overlying our hard hearts."

"I suppose next thing, you'll want me to cut down the gum tree," I said facetiously to Mrs. Kelly when we were discussing the make-believe matter.

The gum tree was a giant magnolia. From its branches every evening after dinner, I used to pluck packages of chewing gum for Peter. I have a moderate knowledge of sleight of hand—not to the point of professionalism, but enough to make some of my friends reluctant to play cards with me—and before strolling out to the gum tree, I would palm several packs of gum in different flavors, and then, reaching up into the leaves, or the heart of the great white blossom, produce the requested flavor. It was my biggest thing as a father.

For a few days after the demise of Melvin, interest in make-believe friends was lukewarm, but presently the dinner

150

table raps and whistles resumed, and eventually Richard the Midget could be heard inquiring of Peter what he wanted for Christmas.

The lesson the Melvin matter taught me was not to make heroes of rascals. Because Melvin had been so highly regarded, all mice, and even rats and gophers took on the aura of friendship. What I wanted to arrange was a line of demarcation between the Good Guys and the Bad Guys where the garden was concerned.

Lizards, toads and frogs ate insects, and so qualified as Good Guys. It occurred to me that while there was plenty of material available on garden pests, very little got into print on the subject of beneficial insects.

Some particularly vicious-looking beetles were really Good Guys because they killed off garden enemies. But how to tell the difference? Has anyone spoken out in print for the Good Guys?

32   What's Bugging You?

I learned early that the best thing you can do for your plants is to find out who their friends are. This isn't as simple as it sounds. There are numerous books and government pamphlets available on insect pests and how to do away with them, but nobody seems interested in accentuating the positive.

Even our good friends at the Farm and Home Advisors Bureau, when asked for material that would help us recognize the good insects, noted briefly but firmly at the bottom of the form letter accompanying the booklet, *Insects and Diseases of Vegetables:* "Sorry, nothing informative is available on the beneficial insects."

Is that any way to treat a ladybug? Or a caterpillar hunter or cicada killer?

The simple truth is, most gardeners think the only good bug is a dead one. They rarely give any thought to the insect benefactors that go on their purposeful way clamping their powerful mandibles around aphids, picnicking on carrion, anesthetizing and stowing away garden vandals, and generally making themselves useful—against terrific odds.

The subject came up one morning when Peter discovered a strange looking beetle walking along the garden hose.

I was all for wiping him out with one stamp of the foot.

"What do you want to kill him for?" Peter demanded. "He's not doing anything."

"Not now, he isn't." I looked around for something to back me up. At that time, I didn't have to look far. "All those holes in the lettuce are probably some of his work."

"Maybe he didn't do it," suggested the *amicus curiae*. "Maybe he's one of the Good Guys."

We got down on our knees and took a closer look. He was a black beetle with red marks, and businesslike mandibles. We scooped him into a bottle for safe keeping, and took off for the library.

That was where we discovered a book that should be in every gardener's library—or preferably in a more handy spot, such as tool house or potting shed. *Insects: A Guide to Familiar American Insects*, by Herbert S. Zim and Clarence Cottam, is the instant bug book for the hurried and harried gardener.

As soon as we got home we ran down the list of beetles, found some with red markings that didn't qualify on other points, and at last came across a mug shot of the prisoner.

It would be gratifying to be able to report that he was a friend of man and garden, highly beneficial to crops—a dedicated destroyer of aphids and spittlebugs.

Unfortunately he turned out to be an asparagus beetle, and up to no good.

However, by thus leading us down the garden path, he had put us onto one of the most fascinating sidelines of gardening. The study of bugs and beetles can introduce you to some amazing and distinctive characters. You will find out that some of the toughest looking ones have the best intentions, and vice versa.

Crickets, for instance, those peaceful sounding musicians, like to munch on your vegetables between performances, and aren't averse to a spot of cannibalism for an encore, now and then. Field crickets are high on the farmers' Bad Guy list.

However, tradition is hard to overcome, and I have never been able to build up the proper amount of antagonism to crickets. I would undoubtedly be able to manage it if I were a farmer with a large tract of land being invaded by them, but as it is, I weigh the peaceful pleasures of the cricket's evening concert against the possibility of his having a midnight snack in my vegetable garden, and call it even.

After all, what if I want to know how hot it is one evening, and am too lazy to look at the thermometer? The tree cricket will tell me the temperature. All I have to do is count the number of chirps or pulsations it emits in a minute, divide by four and add forty.

One of the strongest points against insecticides is that in the garden shoot-out, the good guys get knocked off in the cross fire.

It makes you stop and think. Something ought to be done for the sober, industrious citizens of bug-and-beetledom, so that they might at least have the chance to advance and be recognized.

We were amazed, when we got down to it, to find out how many beneficial insects there are.

154

There are the lacewings whose larvae feed on aphids, earning themselves the businesslike name of aphid lion. Each exemplifies its name. The adult lacewing comes in two sizes and colors; the golden-eye is the larger, with gauzy green wings, and the brown lacewing features beige wings, and is slightly smaller. The larvae are ferocious-looking, flattish, with tufted body and highly functional mandibles.

It turned out that the grayish flies we took for houseflies out in the garden were not bad guys at all, but good guys, or tachinid flies, out gunning for squashbugs and moth larvae. They lay their eggs in the victims, and the young feed off the host.

Even wasps went on the Good Guy list when we discovered that they prey on caterpillars and beetle larvae. The potter wasp and the mud dauber now have right of way through the garden—not that we ever argued with them, but at least we now stepped aside without resentment. It's surprising how your attitude can mellow when you know they may be en route to paralyze a caterpillar busily demolishing a tomato plant.

What really bugged us was that there was such vast and widespread indifference to these garden benefactors.

Their efficiency and ingenuity in trapping their victims, their purposefulness as they stowed them in the bug deep freeze to supply the winter larder or keep the nursery stocked were a never-ending source of wonder. Maybe that is the commodity we have run out of—wonder.

The ant lion is as interesting to study as his animal prototype, and a backyard safari is a lot simpler. They are similar in their entrapment systems to the tiger beetles, whose larvae, the ones you used to call "doodle-bugs" when you

155

were a kid, dig pits and wait cannily to grab the fumble-footed insect passerby. Ant lions prefer to eat ants, but they will gladly make substitutes on the menu. Any small insect who blunders in is welcome.

Then there are the sanitary engineers: both the carrion and rove beetles, a sort of six-legged clean-up squad. They are cousins of the burying or sexton beetle, that excavates the earth under dead animals or insects so that the body falls into the ground, literally burying itself and becoming food for the beetle larvae.

If anything demonstrates the balance in nature, it is a study of the beneficial versus the destructive insects.

Most of us recognize the ladybug (or ladybird), who, it seems, isn't a bug at all, but a beetle (the difference between beetles and bugs being that beetles have biting mouth parts, and bugs have sucking beaks).

Peter's way of fixing the difference in his mind was a variation on the ancient joke:

"Who was that ladybug I saw you with, last night?"
"That was no bug, that was a beetle."

The citrus industry alone owes a tremendous debt of gratitude to this ladybird beetle, which keeps the cottony-cushion scale under control. It takes something like three thousand of these small insects per acre to control the scale pest.

The name, ladybird beetle, goes back to the Middle Ages, when it was dedicated to the Virgin Mary. I have come across this little story in several books, but no one ever seems to know the why and wherefore.

156

In the garden shoot-out, the fastest draw on six legs is the caterpillar hunter, or ground beetle, cousin to the tiger beetle, who is no slouch either, when it comes to speed, but no match for the caterpillar hunter where weapons are concerned.

The caterpillar hunter not only feeds on insects, especially the larvae of the destructive tent caterpillar, and the gypsy moth, but squirts a fluid on his victims, to daze or anesthetize them. They aren't too careful to distinguish between you and lesser victims, so stay out of firing range.

Mantises, which are Good Guys, we had confused with walking sticks who are Bad Guys. We had encountered the latter, and spared them because they were too intriguing-looking to kill. However, we soon found out the difference—walking sticks can damage locust, cherry, oak and walnut trees. Mantises feed principally on insect pests.

Dragonflies are Good Guys, eating small insects; fireflies and their larvae also feed on small bugs and beetles.

The cicada killer is a large wasp, which lives up to its name by paralyzing cicadas with a stinger, and storing them tidily in the deep freeze, thus guaranteeing a constant supply of fresh meat.

Bees, aside from their honey-making propensities, are benefactors, for the obvious reason of pollination. Without their vital work, we would have few plants of any kind, and the other Good Guys would have an unemployment problem.

(Not all bees make honey, but all feed on nectar and perform the pollination service in the process.)

Some of the garden Good Guys aren't insects. Don't forget to include birds, toads and lizards—all insectivorous, and

157

all beneficial to a degree. My amiability toward the feathered Good Guys varies with the amount of their depradations on the fruit. However, weigh their value as insect eaters against the damage to fruit, and they come out as Good Guys.

I protect ripening fruit by tying little plastic sandwich bags over the branch. For still better coverage, save your plastic bags from the cleaner's.

The lizard's talent for growing a new tail from the stub of the old one put them high on the plus side with Peter, even out-weighing their insect-eating proclivities. What the purpose of this disposable tail is, I have never read, although the *Encyclopedia Britannica* in commenting that it surprises and confuses assailants, makes sense to me. It's unnerving enough for humans to observe the phenomenon. I can remember my horror when I was a child, and a lizard's tail came off in my hand.

Of course the list of Good Guys in your garden will depend on what part of the country you live in. Find out which ones are indigenous to your location, and support your local insect friends.

33   Good Guys vs. the Bad Guys

It's relatively easy, and good fun as well, to create your own gallery of the Good Guys of the insect world.

This is a great ready reference guide, and with a reasonable amount of attention to detail and color, it can even be an attractive addition to workshop or potting shed. If yours is like the average shed, it would probably benefit from anything that distracts the eye from sacks, tools and pots.

In learning to recognize the Good Guys of the garden, we found ourselves constantly having to look them up for verification. It was Peter who came up with the idea of a picture gallery of beneficial insects—sort of a rogues gallery in reverse.

This can be a constructive and amusing winter project, and one of its advantages is that you don't have to be a twentieth century Fabre to do it.

What you want is a recognizable portrait, to check against

the original. After all, the bug doesn't care how he looks. But it is important to know, for your garden's sake, just what the insects have in mind.

Paper plates, the ones with fluted rims, make effective backings for the portraits, either concave or convex, depending on whether you use the front or the back. For hanging them, use thumbtacks, or the adhesive hangers from any hardware or dime store.

Our list of friendly insects came to an even dozen, with the inclusion of one non-insect, the earthworm, who we felt rated a place in the gallery regardless of his classification (purely a courtesy on our part).

Of course, if you need a picture of an earthworm in order to recognize one when you meet, you're in trouble.

We made our sketches from color plates in encyclopedias and from drawings in insect books. This is a good way to fix all the details in your mind. Next to a personal encounter with the business end of a bee or a wasp or a beetle (which in the latter case may be both ends, since the tiger beetle and the ground beetle would as soon squirt as bite), I know of nothing that makes an insect more memorable than drawing it yourself.

We found it easier to work on flat sheets of drawing paper, rather than directly on the paper plate. The drawings were then cut out in circles the size of the plate center, and put on with rubber cement.

The name of the insect as well as that of its larva (not always the same, as in the case of the lacewing and its larva, the aphid lion) was placed at the top in india ink.

You may find yourself developing hidden talents in the art line, as you work. On the other hand, you may discover

160

you have no aptitude for the thing at all. If the latter is the case, forget the art gallery, and just post a list of Good Guys for ready reference, giving distinctive points and characteristics.

There's no point in trying to reproduce the subject artistically if you are so inept that you may wind up picking the wrong ones out of the Line-Up.

Our gallery included the following, not all of whom we had the pleasure of meeting in person (due no doubt to the quantities of insecticides in general use, which kill off the innocent with the guilty).

ant lion	earthworm
bee	firefly
carrion beetle	lacewing or aphid lion
caterpillar hunter	ladybird or ladybug
(or ground beetle)	mantis
dragon fly	mud wasp
	tachinid fly

There was some debate as to whether ants deserved a place in the Good Guys Gallery, since some species are beneficial—the Formica rufa, found in pine forests, preys on beetle and insect larvae which damage the trees.

However, since the cornfield ants maintain "herds" of aphids because they have a fancy for the aphid's "milk," we decided to leave ants out of the gallery.

We didn't bother with a Rogues Gallery. If we couldn't match up an insect with a portrait in the Good Guys gallery, we figured he was a Bad Guy, and our policy was, THROW THE RASCALS OUT!

Hanging was too good for 'em.

161

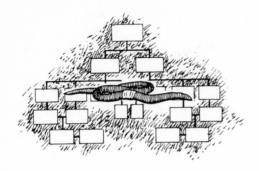

34 Worms, and the Rich, Full Life

If Edwin Markham's "Man With the Hoe" had only under-stood earthworms, he wouldn't have been leaning on that hoe, "bowed by the weight of centuries." He would have been sitting in his cottage doorway quaffing the nut-brown ale, and letting the earthworms do his tilling, or a goodly portion of it.

For singlemindedness and pure love of labor, nothing and nobody can equal earthworms. They have a job and they do it. Don't take my word for it. Darwin wrote of them, "It may be doubted whether there are many other animals which have played so important a part in the history of the world as have these lowly organized creatures."

If ever there was an organization man, it's the earthworm. They even dig in concert. Toss a bunch of them into a box of soil, and watch.

By the simple biologic processes of eating, digesting and eliminating, they add to the supply of gardener's gold called humus.

No lying around in the nursery sucking on pacifiers, or roaring to be picked up. No glooming around in clumps, wondering who they are or why they were born—earthworms *know*. They are here to make humus. That's their bag.

There is only one catch—they can't take bad or sterile material, soil with a minimum of organic content, and turn it into rich soil. Nobody's perfect.

There exists a certain amount of argument, not to say controversy, as to the relative value of the earthworm. Soil experts are now on the fence, some being of the opinion that it is a fallacy that earthworms are necessary to plant growth or to improve the soil, but they admit that they probably add to its value. "I wouldn't want to give you the idea that there might be great advantages in having earthworms," one said cautiously to me. "On the other hand. . . ."

The earthworm man, however, will give measure for measure in the Great Earthworm Controversy. He will point out that the earthworm, by the simple process of eating, digesting and excreting, is a vital factor in the production of humus.

Darwin considered the earthworm valuable enough to rate a book. His *The Formation of Vegetable Mould Through the Action of Earthworms, With Observations on Their Habits* is a convincer. (Don't say you haven't time to read; if you have time to read the title, the book doesn't take much longer.)

He describes the talents of the earthworm in these words:

Worms prepare the ground in an excellent manner for the growth of fibrous rooted plants and for seedlings of all kinds. They periodically expose the mould to the air and sift it so that no stones larger than the particles which they can swallow are left in it.

They mingle the whole intimately together like the gardener who prepares fine soil for his choicest plants. . . . The bones of dead animals, the harder part of insects, the shells of land molluscs, leaves, twigs, etc. are before long all buried beneath the accumulated castings of worms, and are thus brought in a more or less decayed state within reach of the roots of plants. . . .

In short, I don't know of any other animal that asks so little and gives so much. All the earthworm asks is a place to work, enough organic matter to keep body and gizzard together (they do have a gizzard-like arrangement that enables them to grind up bits of gravel and even small stones) and the privilege of doing their thing. To the earthworm, this is fulfillment.

Through the kind offices of the farm advisor, I got in touch with a lady earthworm dealer. She listened to my problem, and advised me against my original plan, which was to buy the largest, fiercest, most aggressive worms she had in stock. Among the numerous colloquial names of earthworms, I had been impressed by the term "night lion," because of its note of vigor and determination, qualities which I knew were vital in any worm confronted with the soil in my back yard.

"Buy bed run," she advised me. "That's assorted sizes, rather than all one size. If you start off with a couple of pounds, including eggs, you will soon have a plentiful supply."

"How do I care for them?" I asked.

"Just loosen up your ground and put them in with some garbage or compost or organic fertilizer. Keep it loose and wet—that's about all there is to it, unless you're going into earthworm culture, with an eye to increasing your stock substantially."

It turned out that the going rate for bed run is two dollars a pound. They are shipped in cups, running roughly fifty-five to a cup, and around 500 to a pound.

Considering the longevity of earthworms when properly cared for, the investment was extremely reasonable, I thought. In my research on the earthworm, I had come up with the startling fact that some have been known to live as long as fifteen years.

Of course, putting yourself in the situation of the average earthworm, the thought inevitably arises, who cares about longevity if all you are is an earthworm? However, since the earthworm doesn't go in for deep thoughts or searching its id, this has never posed any philosophical or psychological problems.

Peter and I, in assessing the rather complicated plans we were making for the garden, figured that we might as well add earthworm culture to horticulture, rather than just tossing the newly acquired stock into the earth, willy-nilly.

We put our mixed bed run into two locations: one, directly into the ground with some compost, from where they could move in any direction they chose.

The other half, or clump, as the dealer called it, we placed in a special culture box—a tomato lug which we bought from the grocery store. We set the box on a support or base, of 2 by 6 foot boards, so that it stood off the ground, to facilitate drainage and prevent the occupants from escaping. Our idea was to construct a nursery, or wormery (since a place where frogs gather is called a froggery, wormery seemed to us an appropriate term for a gathering of worms) modeled roughly along the lines of the breeding boxes where we had acquired our stock.

We filled the box with a mixture of compost, horse manure, topsoil, peat moss and cornmeal (which it seems, increases egg production) and then added the worms, covering them snugly with a wet gunny sack, after they had dug in. This was to keep the ground from drying out.

Gunny sacks, we found, were hard to come by. We had to go over to Hollywood to a feed, grain and coal supply house.

The whole investment ran around $4.75—an amount I did not feel it necessary to report to my business manager. It had been hard enough explaining kumquats. What his reaction might have been to: *earthworms, $4, gunny sacks, 40¢ and one box cornmeal, 35¢*, I didn't even like to think about. It probably wasn't deductible, anyway.

35   Tell Me All About It

It was while I was in the process of discovering the importance and relative scarcity of the earthworm that I ran into
the image thing again.

I was having lunch with a feature writer for a woman's
magazine, and the studio publicist, whose function was to
"cover" the interview. This is the watchdog process by which
the publicist sits warily in a corner of the booth, toying with
drink and salad, assessing every word that issues from actor
or interviewer.

He may look relaxed, even indifferent and a little bored,
but in reality, every mental muscle is tensed and ready to
spring.

If the interviewer should ask a question that the inter-
viewee might conceivably fumble (Is Mr. X really a bum to
work with? Is it true that your co-star in your last film had
a big thing going with the director?) the publicist is ready
with verbal rapier, to intercept, thrust or parry.

This particular interview seemed a safe and fairly innocuous one, the publication being known for sentimental pieces dealing with the homelife of the stars, wherein babies, recipes and cookouts were very large—often considerably larger than life.

"I understand you are an avid gardener," the interviewer began. She was, I felt sure, thinking in terms of rare orchids and prizewinning roses. "What do you raise?"

No matter how you elocute them, cabbage, kale, squash and carrots never come out on the glamour side. I ran down the list with the feeling that I was betraying the magazine readers of America.

The publicist sipped his martini and looked depressed.

I went into the reasons for the vegetable garden, the improvement in Peter's eating habits and the father-son aspects of the situation. She began scribbling delightedly, uttering occasional squeaks and murmurs of approval.

From there we got into fig, apricot, peach, apple and grape country, and the vineyard, which at that time encompassed two vines. Real family magazine stuff. (Not, perhaps, the rugged ranch style material the publicist would have preferred, with range wars and cattle rustlers, but great for the family trade.)

"Now!" she said brightly, "our readers would be thrilled, I know, to hear all about what a movie star does in a typical day away from the glitter and glamour of the sound stage. They think of you not only as a sophisticated star of romantic comedies, but as a rugged outdoor man; and your enthusiasm for the land, the savage struggle to wrest from the earth the very food you eat. . . ."

168

The waiter appeared as though on cue, with a menu filled with suggestions as to the food *we* were going to eat. After we had ordered, the interviewer made a few unsuccessful grabs at the sentence she had dropped, consulted her notes and cried triumphantly, ". . . oh, yes . . . what a movie star does when he isn't making movies! *Now!* Please tell me, for our readers, what you did yesterday, for instance. Tell me all about it!" she commanded eagerly.

My trouble is, when someone says tell me all about it, I take them literally.

The previous day had been almost completely devoted to acquiring earthworms.

"Let me see," I muttered. "Well, if you're sure that's what your readers want. . . ."

I settled down to a session of total recall that was destined to remain with all three of us for some time.

As I opened my mouth, I was aware in the semidarkness of the restaurant, that a pencil was waggling about four inches east of my nose.

"If you don't mind," said the interviewer, "I am going to digress for just a moment. We are going to be running a feature on Christmas gifts. You know, 'What famous people want for Christmas' . . . not the intangibles like world peace, or a little child's laughter, though we did a sweet, *sweet* feature on that, last year. But this time we mean the actual things you might like to find under the Christmas tree. Even something rather unusual. . . ."

"Well, actually," I began thoughtfully, "I happen to know what my son is giving me. He doesn't know I know it, but I heard him ordering it yesterday."

"*That's* the kind of thing we want," she encouraged me, pencil poised. I could see her mentally working out the head: GLENN FORD'S MOST PRECIOUS GIFT.

The publicist was staring off into space with the glazed look in his eyes that denoted peace and safe territory.

"Well, actually, it's a pound of worms," I said.

"*Worms!*" She stared at me, and the glazed look in the publicist's eyes broke up into splinters of alarm.

"That's right," I confirmed. "We've been looking around for a place that sells earthworms—very good for the soil. We found out about this farm that raises them commercially, and Pete's having a box of their finest stock gift wrapped for me, for Christmas."

She thought this over. Then she nodded, and began to make a few notes. "That's . . . well, it's touching," she said. In the fitful candlelight it actually looked as though her eyes were misting. "For the man who has everything . . . yes, that just *might* make a very *tender* and *touching* little *piece*. Thank you, Mr. Ford."

The publicist gave a sigh of relief and settled lovingly down with his martini.

"Now!" the interviewer resumed brightly, "let's get into A Day in the Life of a Movie Star. For instance, let's take yesterday, from the time you got up, right on through. Where did you go? What did you do? Tell me all about it!"

"Well, as a matter of fact," I said cautiously, "we spent the morning out in the valley. Peter and I drove out to this farm—this earthworm farm."

"For goodness' sake," she murmured, scribbling diligently, "you mean it's actually a business?"

"Absolutely. They do an enormous business, supplying

earthworms to ranchers. The demand is tremendous, and there are not many competitors."

"Think of it!" she breathed, writing briskly, "I suppose they are always working to improve the stock—just like with cattle and blooded horses."

"Exactly." I warmed to my subject, encouraged by her interest. I was just starting on the name varieties when the waiter set his serving tray down.

"I did a little research," I explained, "in order to learn just which types would be advantageous to a city garden. The rainworm or *lumbricus terrestris*, and the brandling, or *helodrilus foetidus* are the best from a practical standpoint. . . ."

"My goodness!" she chirruped, "you even know their scientific names! Don't go too fast. How do you spell helo . . . whatever it is. (I bet you're the only movie star in Hollywood with pedigreed earthworms in his garden!) What do the Latin names mean?"

I didn't think this was the time to explain that *helodrilus foetidus* meant stinking earthworm, because of its skunk-like reaction to being annoyed or injured.

"Oddly enough, one of the names for the common earthworm is 'night lion,' " I said hastily.

"IN-teresting," she murmured. "How do they, uh, come . . . I mean how do you buy them? By the inch?" She laughed gently at her little joke.

"That might run into money," I said. "Some rainworms grow as long as twelve inches. Actually, they're sold by the pound, or the clump, as they say in the trade."

The publicist made a worried noise and stared into his pot roast and noodles, which had perhaps been an unfortunate choice.

171

"It's really quite a big business," I said. "The breeders ship them all over the country—they ship them in cups."

The waiter chose this moment to pour the coffee. The interviewer pushed hers away with a listless hand.

I was beginning to feel like a driver going the wrong direction on a freeway. I couldn't turn around, and it didn't seem a good idea to keep on going.

"How much do they cost?" she asked. This seemed a fairly safe question.

"Two dollars a pound. They run around five hundred to the pound—or clump, as they call it. That's including the eggs."

I heard a gulping sound on my right, and the earnest voice of the watchdog. "Another martini," he said to the waiter, "and make it a double."

"Well, well!" said the lady interviewer. "So that was the day *this* movie star had! Now, after you and little Peter got home. . . ." She gave me a look of triumph, having gotten us off the worm farm, and God knows nobody was more grateful than I was, unless it was the publicist. "What did you do then?"

"We added them to the garden soil," I said. I had lost all enthusiasm for the whole project. "You just dig a hole and bury them with some garbage or compost. Keep the soil loose and wet. That's all there is to it," I concluded miserably.

The publicist's voice broke the silence with the force of a sledge hammer.

"Say! With all this talk about . . . uh, gardens, and things, I bet your readers would like a photographic tour of Glenn's house and his garden. Why don't we take a run out to. . . ."

It was unfortunate that the waiter at this moment set in front of the interviewer the dish she had ordered some twenty minutes earlier. A steaming plate of vermicelli.

She gave it a long, slow look. Then she glanced at her watch, reached for her handbag and rose.

"*Look* at the time!" she cried hoarsely. "I wonder if perhaps we could conclude the interview some other day, and discuss the possibility of a house and garden layout at the same time. Right now I have to fly!"

She flew.

Times have changed. If the interview had taken place today, the magazine would have come up with a story on *The Love Life of the Earthworm as Explained by Glenn Ford.* They'd have gotten *something* out of it.

As it was, the lady interviewer never got around to doing the feature or the layout, and come to think of it, the Christmas item never made it either.

It was obvious that she equated me with the dictionary's secondary definition of *earthworm:* "a mean, sordid person."

36   The Lowly Mushrump

A strange looking thing had appeared on one of the pines on the slope behind our late poultry house.

It was a wide, white growth, clammy to the touch, and a little on the sinister-looking side.

"Don't touch it!" Mrs. Kelly ordered Peter, who had discovered it. "And go wash your hands," she added, with a woman's knowledge of the child mind, which told her he had examined it before revealing it to adults.

"Gosh, it won't poison you if you just touch it!" he complained.

"You don't *know* that. It's prob'ly something to do with all those underground blasts," she added darkly.

"Nonsense," I said, "it's a fungus of some kind."

George, passing by with a load of leaves for the compost heap, gave the Thing a cursory glance. "It's a oyster mushrump," he announced.

"It's just as eatable as them things." He pointed to a cluster of small egg-shaped mushrooms under the trees.

"I wouldn't have 'em in my kitchen," said Mrs. Kelly. "A cousin of mine's best friend ate one of them and she was dead on the floor when they found her."

George was squatting by the cluster on the ground. "These are mushrumps—Inky Caps."

Mrs. Kelly returned to the house, looking unconvinced. Peter and I got down on our knees for a closer look.

"Don't eat 'em if you're gonna have a drink before," George said.

"Why's that?" I wondered, realizing that this was the first really sustained conversation I had ever had with the uncommunicative George.

He shrugged. "I dunno. That's what they say."

"You sure know a lot about . . . uh . . . mushrumps," Peter commented, impressed.

"I *better* know about 'em," snorted George. "Me and my brother-in-law, we're going into the mushrump business together. Starting next month."

That was how we learned that George was leaving.

I was so filled with the glow of well-being with which sudden good news infuses us that I listened fascinated to every word he spoke, which turned out to be quite a few.

Peter's friend Norman, drawn by the radar that conveys any news of an unusual or morbid nature, came to inspect the strange growth.

"What you gotta do, you gotta study 'em," George said, lifting one of the egg-shaped mushrooms from its moorings. "You could eat mosta the mushrumps you see around. Just learn about the ones that are eatable, so's you can recognize

175

'em. These Inky Caps, you gotta pick 'em and cook 'em before they turn black and kinda inky."

"Oh, boy!" said Peter, "I'm gonna have me a ink sandwich!"

"You could grow your own mushrumps if you like 'em that well," George suggested. "All you need is a place that's dark enough and damp enough. . . ."

"We could *sell* 'em!" said Peter, always the business man.

Norman hit him a whack on the arm. "Our school project!" he yelled. "We have to have a commercial project and report on it every week. That's what we'll have, a mushroom project!"

"Well, of course you got to have the right kinda compost, and temper'ture control," George said doubtfully. "It's not all that easy."

"We could grow 'em in the closet in my room," Peter suggested.

"Well, that's not exactly. . . ." I began.

"I got just the place!" Norman yelped. "My father had this atomic bomb shelter built a long time ago, and we never even used it." His voice indicated extreme disappointment that the anticipated need had never arisen. "My father hardly ever even goes into it—except maybe when my married sister brings her kids over to our house. . . ."

"Go ask your father if he would object, Norman," I suggested.

"He's at his office," Norman told me, with a look that said any normal father would be similarly occupied. "C'mon, Pete, we'll go look at it."

I made a mental note to go and get some books on the subject of mushroom growing. Meanwhile it seemed a good idea to get all the information I could from George.

176

He turned out to be a well of information that would never run dry.

Mushrooms, it appeared, could be and were being grown in such diverse places as abandoned mines, cellars, and barns. But George and his brother-in-law were using the more conventional mushroom houses, having acquired a converted factory which approximated the requirements as to space, location and structure.

I had never thought of mushrooms as being particularly valuable from a nutrition standpoint, but now I learned that their protein, vitamin and mineral content was considerable. George was tossing around words like pantothenic acid and riboflavin and thiamin with the assurance of a health food addict.

It occurred to me that I was witnessing the transformation of a man who had found his right work.

"Know what I like about mushrumps?" he demanded abruptly. "I like 'em because they don't need no mowing and pruning and transplanting. And you don't have to rake up no leaves from mushrumps, either.

"And another thing, you don't have to muck around outside all the time, except for the composting. And there's machines for that. First thing you do is make up that compost. You get piles of horse manure, maybe eight, ten feet high, six or seven feet acrost. Keep it wet, real wet. Then you add gypsum, about maybe thirty pounds to a ton of manure."

"That's a lot of manure, all right," I said.

"That's *right!*" George said. "A *lotta* manure. Then two, maybe four days after, you gotta break it all up, wet it down again and get the mixing machine turning it."

177

I began to have doubts about mushroom growing at home. "Well, George," I said, getting briskly to my feet, "it's certainly fine that you're. . . ."

"Now," he went on, "by the time you done all that, you got fermentation—right?"

"I guess so," I said. Where the *hell* were those kids?

"Okay, so your fermentation helps break down your compost. When it's all ready, you're gonna put it in the beds, and the heat of the manure, plus some live steam brings up the temper'ture to around 140 degrees. This is called pasteurizing. It gets rid of your bugs and Nematodes . . . oh, . . . about the compost: sometimes your horse manure is too full of straw, so you gotta add some grain or cottonseed meal or maybe poultry manure, for the nitrogen in 'em. That's if your horse manure is too. . . ."

"Horse manure!" I said. "That reminds me. I better see about getting some on the. . . ."

"Brewers grain," George continued without a pause. "That's a good thing to add. One third at the second turn, and one third at the third turn, and what's left over you put in at the fourth. . . ."

He paused and shook his head. "Some of these growers back east, they're using this sympathetic compost. That means like the real thing, on'y imitation. . . ."

"Oh . . . synthetic!" I said.

"Yeah, sympathetic. It's gotta have a lot more water than your horse manure. A *lot* more water."

"Water!" I cried. "Those strawberries are pretty dry. . . ."

"You know another reason why I'm gonna like this work?"

I grunted. I knew now that nothing short of an act of God or a runaway truck bursting through the shrubbery was

178

going to distract him from recording the joys of mush-rooming.

"I'm gonna tell you why I'm gonna enjoy it," he went on inflexibly, "I'm gonna enjoy it because it's my business—half of it, anyways. I put my nest egg into that business, and every damn mushrump comes outa those sheds—every 'break' —that's what they call it when they come through the beds— why, I can say fifty percent of those mushrumps belong to me!" Then, thoughtfully, "Do you know the prices on mush-rumps changes so fast it's in the newspapers every day?"

I didn't know this.

"Yessir, just like stocks and bonds. What you do, you turn your mushrumps over to the produce dealers and they charge you a percent for marketing 'em. My brother-in-law's got a deal to sell to a cannery, too.

"Of course, there's a lot can happen . . . you get a hot spell, and every mushrump grower's got a big harvest. And they gotta reach the market the same day they're picked. Still and all. . . ."

It occurred to me that George was going headlong into a highly uncertain situation, dealing with a perishable com-modity on a shifting and capricious market, risking his life savings at a time when he was not a young man. In short, I realized, he was doing the most exciting thing in the world: going whole hog at something that was his own project, and his own risk. And he was a happy man, for the first time since I had known him.

I held out my hand. "George," I said, "I hope the next time I hear from you, sales are mushrooming . . . er, rump-ing."

A slow grin spread across his lined and sunbrowned face.

179

Looking embarrassed but determined, he took a rumpled slip of paper from a back pocket and thrust it at me.

"My sister-in-law, she found this pome in a book, and she wrote it down for me."

He watched as I read the couplet aloud:

> He that high growth on cedars did bestow
> Gave also lowly mushrumps leave to grow.

Robert Southwell, 1561–1575

"I like to read that over every oncet in a while," said George.

37 Time Is a Gentleman

It struck me as rather a nice touch, that the boys were going to raise mushrooms in a place that had been built to shelter people from a mushroom-shaped cloud—the Atomic Age version of beating the swords into plowshares.

I mentioned it to Mrs. Kelly, as I peered into the refrigerator for a before-dinner snack.

"Those kids are going to get a wallop out of having a bomb shelter for their headquarters."

"Every boy needs a secret place of his own," she commented. "Puts me in mind of my brother Everett. He and his pal, Billy Goskins, had this secret place down in a culvert. One day they disappeared, and we hadda get the fire department to dig 'em out. They was pinned down in there by a cave-in."

"A cave-in!" The possibility was not too remote from an old, disused bomb shelter. "Who . . . what . . . did they. . . ."

"Oh, they got 'em out, all safe and sound—well, not exactly *sound*," she added, whipping potatoes vigorously. "Billy got one leg kinda mashed. . . ."

"The bomb shelter is *out!*" I said abruptly as Peter and Norman came in. "No underground projects. If you can find a place that's above ground, and safe. . . ."

"But *you* said we could use the bomb shelter!" Peter argued, with logic.

"Never mind," I said, adding with sudden inspiration, "it would worry me too much when I'm away."

After they had grumbled themselves out of the kitchen, I suddenly thought of the dark room. I used it so rarely that I could certainly spare it for the duration of the mushroom project.

I went out to tell the boys the good news, but they had disappeared.

"Well, you're certainly not going to have them mixing manure in the house, I should hope!" Mrs. Kelly protested.

"I figured out a way to avoid all that mess," I told her, rummaging through a stack of magazines in the den. Somewhere I had seen a full page ad for one of those mail order houses. Here it was.

HOW TO GROW MUSHROOMS IN YOUR OWN CELLAR! IN JUST ONE MONTH YOU CAN SERVE YOUR OWN SUCCULENT, TASTY MUSHROOMS. Be the envy of your friends. No seeds. Nothing to plant. Just send for our unique kit. . . .

I showed it to Mrs. Kelly.

"I'm going to order a kit for each of the boys. This is clean, compact and foolproof."

That, as it turned out, was the trouble with it.

Peter, when I told him what I had done, stared at me with something less than gratitude in his eyes.

"But I want to do it the real way! I don't want something that's all ready and easy. I want to plant 'em and make the manure compost, and pasteurize 'em—and all that stuff George has been telling me and Norm you have to do. It's *my* project! *I* want to do it!"

"Now, Peter," Mrs. Kelly reproached him, "your father wanted to have everything just right for you. . . ."

I shook my head, and followed my son out of the room.

I was thinking not of Peter, but of two Georges. George the gardener and George Bernard Shaw.

I had met Shaw on two occasions. People have asked me, did he say anything witty, or memorable? I don't remember that he did, except that he was sharp, quick-spoken and abrupt. I don't believe all famous writers customarily drop literary words of wisdom in company with people who are not intimates. Most of them are reminiscent of David Garrick's tombstone inscription for Oliver Goldsmith:

. . . who wrote like an angel, and talked like poor Poll.

My keenest memory of GBS was a paragraph from his "Epistle Dedicatory" of *Man and Superman*.

This is the true joy in life, the being used for a purpose recognized by yourself as a mighty one; the being thoroughly worn out before you are thrown on the scrap heap; the being a force of Nature instead of a feverish selfish little clod of ailments and grievances complaining that the world will not devote itself to making you happy.

183

I was realizing that the reason Peter had been so excited about the mushroom project was that it was completely his own idea. Certainly the gardening project was his project too, but initiated by me, promoted by me, and though shared with enthusiastic interest by him, still an extension of an adult plan.

Mushroom raising was solidly his own. Mushrooms were adventure, fraught with the possibility of failure, but shared with someone his own age, with similar reactions and caprices.

And George, the gardener George, he was a happy man because he too was going into something of his devising, demanding hard, unremitting work, and constant supervision, perhaps encompassing failure, or the threat of failure. But still—his own undertaking.

Peter was standing in the garden moodily crunching a raw carrot.

"Here's the key to the darkroom," I said matter-of-factly. "It ought to make a pretty fair place to raise mushrooms."

His face lit up. "You mean we can raise mushrooms the right way? Just Norm and me?"

I nodded.

"Sounds like you're both going to be awfully busy, what with one thing and another," Mrs. Kelly commented from the kitchen window.

"It's all right," I said. "You can always find time for the important things. The things you really want to do. Time is a gentleman—he'll make himself available if you really mean business."

The only thing that was worrying me was the matter

of the compost—a messy proceeding, from what George had said. Even on a small scale. . . .

"Listen!" Peter said, "You know what George said he'd do? He said he'd get us some of that sympathetic compost— then we won't have to have real manure. And we can buy the spawn from him—that's what makes the mushrooms grow. He's going to have to buy a lot, and he said he'll be glad to have us buy some from him. It's only about sixty-five cents a pound. And we get a 10 percent discount."

"What's that sympathetic thing he's talking about?" Mrs. Kelly asked as I passed through the kitchen.

"It's good for mushrooms," I told her. "Makes them grow."

Come to think of it, it does the same for people.